The McGraw-Hill Homeschooling Companion

✔ Laura Saba
✔ Julie Gattis

D0557165

McGraw-Hill

New York   Chicago   San Francisco   Lisbon   London
Madrid   Mexico City   Milan   New Delhi
San Juan   Seoul   Singapore
Sydney   Toronto

McGraw-Hill

A Division of The McGraw·Hill Companies

1 2 3 4 5 6 7 8 9 0   DOC/DOC   0 9 8 7 6 5 4 3 2

ISBN 0-07-138617-3

This book was set in Janson by North Market Street Graphics

Printed and bound by R. R. Donnelley & Sons Company.

This publication is designed to provide accurate and authoritative information in regard to the subject matter covered. It is sold with the understanding that the publisher is not engaged in rendering legal, accounting, or other professional service. If legal advice or other expert assistance is required, the services of a competent professional person should be sought.

—From a declaration of principles jointly adopted by a committee of the American Bar Association and a committee of publishers.

This book is printed on recycled, acid-free paper containing a minimum of 50% recycled, de-inked fiber.

For Brandon and Christopher Ojaste,
who have brought such joy to my life.

—Laura Saba

For Mike, Martin, Madeleine, Isabel, and Ross.

—Julie Gattis

Contents

Foreword

If you had mentioned homeschooling to someone a few years ago, you would probably conjure images of an overseas missionary, a cult indoctrinating pliable young minds, or a scofflaw secretly huddled over the kitchen table. Indeed, until recently homeschooling was an underground movement, illegal or difficult in most states.

If you mention homeschooling to someone today, you probably elicit conflicting images of respect and concern. Respect, because home-schooled students achieve beyond expectation. They rapidly advance to one to three years beyond their age peers in public schools. They consistently win national competitions such as the national spelling bee, geography contest, and mathematics olympiad, and they do well on standardized tests including college entrance examinations. Concern, because there still is a great deal of ignorance about homeschooling. The image is still one of cloistered, one-on-one instruction huddled over the kitchen table.

As one of the more visible researchers who has studied homeschooling, I have had the good fortune to meet a great number of homeschool families and homeschool students. Personally, I have been awestruck. I have found the kids to be intelligent, quietly confident, and quite sociable. I have been most impressed by the students' ability to think for themselves, use resources, and plan activities, and especially by their love of learning. In my mind, the success of these students underscores several things that the educational research community has known all along. First, kids have amazing potential. With the right environment and right encouragement, they can do exceptionally well. Second, the things that public school teachers have wanted all along—small classrooms, ability to customize the curriculum, dedicated parents, minimal disciplining events, more field trips, more practical material, time to allow children to pursue their interests, and less bureaucracy—help children achieve. Homeschools have these things in abundance.

I am awestruck as well by the parents. This is a major commitment that has radically affected their children's lives. How did they get started? What went through their minds? Where did they get help? There were a thousand questions I wanted to ask homeschool parents and probably several more thousand that I didn't know I should ask. I did ask hundreds. But homeschooling is a private event born out of parents' love and dedication to their children. The commitment is made at the risk of incurring aspersions and constantly having to defend one's actions. I could only ask a fraction of the questions I wanted to know as a researcher.

If you are a parent contemplating homeschooling or one who is deeply immersed in the activity, there are thousands of practical and psychological questions that must be going through your mind. That's where this book fits in. *The McGraw-Hill Homeschooling Companion* is a major compilation of practical, no-nonsense advice concerning the nuts and bolts of homeschooling. It is such a major compilation that it is like being in a room with 100 homeschool veterans, being able to ask any question that crosses your mind and learning more than you ever expected.

After carefully reading this foreword, I suggest starting this book by looking at the appendixes. First you will find synopses of the state laws so you can learn your legal obligations. You will then see a massive list of national and state organizations dedicated to homeschooling. You will learn that there are many specialized organizations whose mission is to provide support and help you succeed. Most likely there is an organization of like-minded homeschoolers in your region. You should go to some of the provided Web addresses and investigate some of these organizations.

With the large number of homeschool families, homeschooling has substantial market power. The third appendix is an annotated list of hundreds of suppliers of books, software, and other materials targeted to the homeschool market. The fourth appendix provides an organized list of hundreds of useful websites. The last appendix is a brief listing of a scope and sequence of what is often covered in each grade and subject.

After perusing the appendixes, you should be impressed by the breadth and depth of resources that you have available to help with your homeschooling efforts.

Next, you should look at the Contents. The authors tell you the practical side of homeschooling. They help you identify and think through the issues. Remember the thousand questions you wanted to ask and the thousands that you didn't know enough to ask? This powerful resource answers those questions—everything including self-appraisal, mission clarification, responding to neighbors, creating a learning environment, lesson plans, support groups, and tools of the trade.

Homeschooling is not easy, but *The McGraw-Hill Homeschooling Companion* makes starting and maintaining a homeschool much easier.

LAWRENCE M. RUDNER, Ph.D., M.B.A.
Director, ERIC Clearinghouse on Assessment and Evaluation
University of Maryland, College Park

Acknowledgments

Many people have contributed to our book, either through direct assistance or through their loving and generous support. We would like to thank the following:

Nancy Love, our agent, whose dedication to this project from the beginning helped bring it to fruition; Barbara Gilson, our editor at McGraw-Hill, who generously provided both her support and faith in this project, guiding us with her wisdom and experience every step of the way; and Dr. Lawrence Rudner, who graciously dedicated his time and effort to writing our foreword. We would also like to thank those who blazed the trail before us, making homeschooling an increasingly more viable and popular option, including: Micki and David Colfax, Dr. Raymond Moore, John Holt, Mary Pride, John Taylor-Gatto, Rebecca Rupp, and Cafi Cohen.

Laura Saba would like to further express thanks for the support of Brandon and Christopher Ojaste, for their continuing love and patience; mom, dad, Mary Ellen, Anthony, and Tom, for their love and encouragement; Serena Dean, for not only her gift of friendship, but for a million other things along the way; Mark J. Melaccio, for his tremendous love and faith, even in the most difficult times; Mary Heuer McGee, for her gifts of friendship and wisdom; Laura LoBianco, for her friendship and encouragement; Christopher Little, who with one small sentence about "pluck" changed my life forever; and finally, to Julie Gattis, my coauthor.

Why Homeschool?

The recent media coverage of homeschooling may have grabbed your attention. Perhaps you have an acquaintance or two who does it. Over the past decade, the homeschooling movement has exploded. In 1990 there were 300,000 homeschooled children, and in 1998 it was estimated that they numbered 1.5 million.

This chapter will help you understand why people are homeschooling, its legal implications, and its historical roots.

Why Do People Homeschool?

In the United States, public school is available free of charge to all children. Children can spend their day getting educated while their parents are out earning a living. It's a logical system. Why on earth would anyone want to homeschool?

There are a variety of reasons parents decide to teach their children at home rather than use the traditional school systems. Homeschooling requires a strong commitment by the parents, and often the reasons behind their decision to homeschool foster such dedication. The following are some of the more common reasons cited by home-schoolers.

Religious Convictions

Many parents are concerned about their child's religious development. For this reason, they may decide to send their kids to parochial school or to homeschool. They want the study of religion to be at the core of their children's educational program, and they are uncomfortable with the prospect of placing their children in the charge of teachers who may not share their faith. Homeschooling solves this problem.

Social Situations

Sometimes parents are frightened by the news coverage of violent incidents in our schools. They worry, too, about their children's exposure to illegal drugs, alcohol, and teen sex. These parents feel that home-schooling gives them more opportunity to guide their teens in making wise decisions about issues that have such a big impact on their lives. They aren't comfortable with having their teens in an environment in which some of their peers are troubled, coming from unhealthy, dysfunctional homes.

Family Values

Homeschooling families are able to spend a lot of time together. Families in which each member goes his or her separate way all day long don't have this opportunity. Many homeschoolers feel that this togetherness promotes a healthy, nurturing environment for children. They often feel that it is a natural function of parents to educate their children and don't wish to delegate this job to others.

Educational Excellence

No matter how fine a job the local school does in educating children, it is still a large institution. Due to the sheer numbers of children in attendance, children cannot possibly get the individual attention they can with homeschooling. The homeschooling parent can capture their children's interest and run with it, allowing their children to learn more than is possible in a classroom setting. This helps keep the children's love of learning alive. If children excel in a particular subject, they can progress to higher levels of work as soon as they are ready.

Personal Educational Philosophy

Many homeschooling parents feel that active little children are not well suited for a classroom setting. They want to be able to structure their children's school day in ways that allow them to be successful. They have their own opinions about what sorts of information should be taught and when. They want the freedom to direct their children's educational program.

Feeling Underserved

Some minority parents feel that their children are not well served by their local school. So they have sought alternative means of educating their children, such as charter schools or homeschooling.

Children with Special Needs

Sometimes parents of gifted children, or of those with learning disabilities, decide to homeschool their children so that the children can reap the benefits of one-on-one tutorial instruction. Children with ADHD may be unable to sit at a desk for the periods of time required in a classroom, but at home, their parents can make adjustments. Teaching learning disabled children at home may also prevent some of the self-esteem problems that occur when children are labeled "different" from their peers. In a homeschool setting, their strengths can be nurtured and reinforced so that they may grow up without ever realizing something is "wrong" with them.

Is It Legal?

Nowadays, many homeschooling parents take their right to homeschool their children for granted. However, states had to fight for these rights. Several U.S. Supreme Court decisions in the 1920s limited the power of states to interfere in the education of children. First in 1919, Nebraska had passed a law prohibiting any school subject from being taught in any language other than English, and foreign language instruction could only be given after completion of the eighth grade.

Mr. Meyer, a teacher in a parochial school, used a book written in German to teach religion and the German language. Meyer was found guilty of teaching a foreign language to a student who had not passed the eighth grade. Meyer challenged on the grounds that the law violated Meyer's right to teach and parents' rights to hire him to teach under the Fourteenth Amendment. The Fourteenth Amendment states that "No state shall make or enforce any law which shall abridge the privileges or immunities of citizens of the United States; nor shall any state deprive any person of life, liberty, or property, without due process of law." The U.S. Supreme Court agreed, and in the case of *Meyer v. Nebraska* reversed the conviction. In 1922 the state of Oregon passed a law requiring all children from ages 8 through 18 to be educated in public schools. Parents who refused to comply would face criminal charges. A group of Catholic schools challenged the law. So, in the case of *Pierce v. Society of Sisters*, the Supreme Court ruled that the law mandating public school attendance was unconstitutional because it unreasonably interfered with the rights of parents to direct the upbringing and education of their children. Then in 1927, in the case of *Farrington v. Tokushige*, the Supreme Court found that a law serving many of the Chinese and Japanese residents that imposed all sorts of regulations on teachers, textbooks, and subjects in private foreign language schools in Hawaii, including specifying what they could and could not teach, was unconstitutional.

The Home School Legal Defense Association (HSLDA), founded in 1983, has been instrumental in the passage of legislation, and today all 50 states have laws permitting homeschooling. Nowadays, most homeschoolers simply do what they need to do to comply with their states' laws and never experience any legal hassles. Some homeschooling parents have not been so fortunate, however. There have been cases of homeschooling parents being charged with the crimes of "educational neglect" or "truancy" for failing to obey their states' compulsory attendance laws. Even though the law allows homeschooling, vague or restrictive laws still occasionally result in parents facing criminal charges. HSLDA has defended many parents throughout the United States who have found themselves in such predicaments. The HSLDA works to protect parents' rights to homeschool their children.

What About Socialization?

How will children become adequately socialized if they spend all day at home rather than in school with their peers? This is perhaps the most frequently asked question about homeschooling. Homeschooling parents believe that socialization of children is a function of the family. They reject the notion that children must spend their day surrounded by age-mates in order to become socialized. Homeschooled children typically have playmates of a range of ages since they haven't learned that all their friends have to be their own age.

Socialization involves learning to interact appropriately with others, and homeschooling parents have plenty of opportunities to facilitate this process. They intervene when their children need assistance in maintaining acceptable behavior. Parents also serve as role models for their children, teaching them many social skills through their example. Children get to observe their parents dealing with a variety of people as they accompany them on the business of day-to-day living. In these ways, homeschooled children learn how to function in society, and this is "real-world" socialization. Peter Kowalke, a junior at Ohio University, is a former homeschooled kid, as is his wife. He writes a column for *Home Education Magazine*, has written numerous homeschooling articles, speaks at homeschooling conferences, and has recently produced a documentary about grown homeschoolers entitled, *Grown without Schooling*. (His work and information about the documentary can be found at unschooler.com.) Parents who are considering homeschooling their children often have concerns about how homeschooled kids fare when they grow up and attend college or enter the workforce with their conventionally schooled peers. We interviewed Peter Kowalke to help address these concerns.

JULIE: From what you gathered from your interactions with a good many grown homeschoolers, can you make some generalizations about how they fare socially once they leave their homeschools and move on?

PETER KOWALKE: I find them to be socially competent people. Homeschoolers don't live in a void, even if they interact with proportionately less people throughout the course of a day. They build more deep, lasting relationships.

A Brief History of Homeschooling

Homeschooling is not an entirely new idea. George Washington learned to read at home before he ever attended school and only attended for two years before his father's death made school financially unfeasible. Abraham Lincoln attended school sporadically and probably not more than a total of a year.

In the late eighteenth century, American public education really got under way, with many communities establishing schools. Horace Mann was an enthusiastic advocate of compulsory schooling. Due to the activism of Mann and others, by the 1840s compulsory attendance laws were emerging. By about 1910 the one-room schoolhouse had largely made way for "factory" schools, age-graded institutions bearing more resemblance to our modern schools. It wasn't until the 1970s that the modern homeschooling movement began. Dissatisfied with schools for a variety of reasons, a few parents started educating their children at home, but homeschooling didn't really gain momentum until the next decade.

From the mid-1980s through the present, the number of homeschoolers has grown considerably. Court challenges and legislation has made homeschooling a legal alternative in all 50 states.

JULIE: How do these adults do in the workplace? Is the homeschooled person able to work well with others, perhaps on a team, and conform to the expectations of the employer?

PETER KOWALKE: Grown homeschoolers perform famously in the workplace. They are generally ideal employees: bright, eager to learn, engaged in the work, responsive, and very hard working. I hear very few complaints about homeschoolers in the workplace—almost nothing negative. The concern that homeschoolers work poorly with others is an amusing myth. Grown homeschoolers are less likely to be self-centered and are often accustomed to strong roles in both family and community. Although many are very independent and entrepreneurial, at the same time they value community and are used to working within community structure. This carries over to teamwork.

JULIE: What are their lives like now? Do they have successful careers?

PETER KOWALKE: Yes, they have successful careers, although they tend to view success in postmaterialist terms; many grown homeschoolers want more than just money and possessions. They pursue personally meaningful work more often than many who attend school and are willing to earn a few less dollars for work that excites and inspires them. In other words, they are more or less happy people doing what they want to do. Grown homeschoolers know how to have their cake and eat it too. Writing about them is very inspirational.

Is Homeschooling for You?

IN THIS CHAPTER

✔ Can you make the commitment?

✔ Are you qualified?

✔ What if both parents work?

✔ How much does it cost to homeschool?

✔ Island of the lost boys

✔ Is your spouse supportive?

✔ Do you have what it takes?

✔ What will the neighbors say?

Homeschooling is a viable option for those willing and able to take on the challenges it presents, but is it right for your family? Unlike other choices parents make about their children's education, the decision to homeschool encompasses a lifestyle change. Whether or not this lifestyle is one that suits your family is a consideration that demands careful thought if you are to pursue it effectively.

Can You Make the Commitment?

This is likely the single most important question for you to consider. Parents who have a strong desire to homeschool their children, coupled with a determination to be successful at it, usually are. Even a lack of credentials and formal teaching experience don't hinder dedicated parents in providing their children with a good education, because parents feel an awesome sense of accountability for their children's success. For the most part, homeschooling parents will find a way to make sure Johnny learns to read, out of parental love for Johnny, but also due to the uncomfortable knowledge that if Johnny doesn't learn to read, the parents will have no one to blame but themselves.

Are You Qualified?

Schoolteachers typically prepare for their jobs through years of academic course work and practical student teaching experiences. So how can parents with no teaching background expect to do a job that others do only after a good deal of formal preparation? We have a couple of answers to that question. The first is that homeschoolers don't do the same job as classroom teachers. A teacher is charged with the monumental task of imparting specific skills and knowledge to a large group of students from varied backgrounds who have a wide range of abilities and learning styles. Some children in the typical classroom will have embraced a love of learning, supported by their parents, while others may come from homes in which parents are too busy struggling to make ends meet or dealing with personal crises to find the time to foster a love of learning in their children.

However, homeschooling parents are fortunate in that they don't have to be able to teach a classroom filled with a diverse group of kids. They only have to manage one or at most several children, and not necessarily all at once if they arrange their day well.

Schoolteachers have to spend a large portion of their classroom time maintaining order and addressing a variety of needs among their students. If a student misbehaves in a way that requires disciplinary action, there are policies and procedures to be followed and the possibility that the parents of the disruptive student won't support the teacher's efforts to improve the child's classroom behavior. The homeschooling parent, on the other hand, can eliminate most discipline problems that might interfere with learning by incorporating some basic skills of good parenting, such as enforcing limits on inappropriate behaviors, developing a firm but kind approach to discipline, and ensuring that the child carry out her responsibilities.

Additionally, schoolteachers have to follow a prescribed program and stay reasonably on schedule. They are under a lot of pressure to teach as efficiently as possible, while trying to pace things so as not to "lose" a faster or slower student along the way. Classroom time is precious, and if a teacher's methods are ineffective, a group of kids might fail to acquire certain skills. The homeschooling parent, on the other hand, doesn't have to work within these time constraints, and no dire consequences occur if the parent's first attempts to teach long division fail dismally. There's plenty of time to try another approach, and the parent can continue to do so until it is mastered, without much worry as to whether he is slowing down others. As you can see, a homeschooling parent can help his children learn without having to worry about many of the issues a schoolteacher must face.

It has been found that one-on-one instruction can usually be accomplished in a fraction of the time needed to teach a diverse group of students the same material, and the parent can adjust the amount of time spent working on the different subjects to best suit the learning needs of his children. If his children have trouble understanding how to do a type of math problem, there's no need to move on to the next concept until the children have mastered the current one.

If you'd like to better prepare yourself, though, do like many homeschooling parents do: read books about homeschooling and talk to experienced homeschoolers to get a feel for how they approach it. Keep your mind open, and be prepared for some trial and error before you discover the method that works best for your family. You may fumble a little, or even a lot, at first, but over time you will come to know your children's academic strengths and weaknesses and realize you've come to know better than anyone else how to reach your children.

Does this mean you are a fully qualified teacher? Yes and no. You likely haven't learned some of what a schoolteacher knows; however, as you have seen, you don't need many of those skills in your circumstances, anyway. So, while you may not be qualified to lead a diverse class in their education, you will discover that the combination of your dedication, enthusiasm, and the right resources can lead you to be a very successful and highly qualified homeschooling parent—and ultimately, this is all the qualification you need.

What if Both Parents Work?

The ideal situation, in most cases, is when one spouse can give up the job and stay home with the children. Look closely at your expenses and think about what they would be if one of you stayed at home. Would you save money by being in a lower tax bracket? Would you save money by making fewer impulse and time-saving purchases when you are tired? Fewer meals out? Lower clothing and dry-cleaning expenses? Sometimes when people examine the expenses they have that are work related, they find they are not really making anywhere near as much money as they thought they were. So, look at all the places you could save money if you were at home, and decide if it is something you can do.

Can it be done if both parents have to continue working? Yes, it can, though in a family with two working parents, homeschooling requires an extremely high level of parental commitment and isn't something that works well for every family. Some couples manage to pull it off very well, but it's quite a challenge. Some of the things they do to be successful include:

• **Staggering Work Schedules.** Can you or your spouse work a second or third shift? Can one of you work a three-day, 36-hour schedule over the weekend? This is a solution some homeschooling families have come up with. If you can adjust your schedules in this way, you can each be responsible for schooling the children on certain days. The positive side of this is that both parents play an active role in schooling the children, which is not always possible for many homeschooling families. The downside is that you will see less of your spouse, but with careful planning, you can still have time together. You just need to make sure you create that time.

• **Self-Employment.** Does one of you work in a field where there is potential for you to become self-employed? If so, you could work from the home, schooling the children in the early morning hours, and working from noon until 7 or 8 p.m. If your children are old enough, they could even help you with the business, getting involved in clerical work and gaining wonderful real-world skills in the process.

• **Job Sharing and Flextime.** Does your company have job sharing and flextime options? If they don't, you should propose it to them.

Many progressive corporations have welcomed these options. How does it work? Job sharing is when you work part time, sharing one position with another part-timer. The two of you work together to make sure the job is done, but it allows each of you to work part time in an otherwise full-time position. Flextime is when a corporation allows you to create your own hours. You may work from noon until 8 p.m. If you and your spouse could work on flextime, you could then stagger your schedules so that you can homeschool.

● **Telecommuting.** Now that we have entered the computer age, more and more people are working from home, using their computer to keep up with what is going on at the office. Computers now have fax capabilities, and when you combine that with e-mail and your telephone, you can oftentimes do all your work from home. Some companies require you to be in the office one day per week, and if that is the case, you can school on a Saturday or Sunday to make up for the lost day during the week.

Explore your options and see what can work for you. With dedication and a little creativity, you can usually work out a solution. If you really want to homeschool, put your mind to it and make it work!

How Much Does It Cost to Homeschool?

Homeschooling can be as inexpensive and, conversely, as expensive as you want to make it. There are books that demonstrate how you can homeschool for almost no cost at all. Or you can buy a complete prepackaged curriculum that comes with everything you need for the school year, right down to the pens and paper. However, a complete prepackaged curriculum can be very expensive, so make sure that is the route you want to take before you embark upon it. You may choose instead to use your library, the Internet, and encyclopedias to their fullest extent, creating units to study, as you can create these for little or no cost.

If you're fortunate in that you don't have to factor in cost, there are many ways to make homeschooling as expensive as you'd like, trust us! You can opt to purchase expensive math manipulatives, readers, and premade science kits, or if you are trying to maintain a tight budget so that you can stay home to homeschool, you can opt to use dry beans,

M&M's, or chocolate chips for the manipulatives and the library for your readers and for books on simple science experiments.

One cost you may want to consider is that of a computer. While it seems like a big expense, it can certainly save a lot of money in the long run. You can allow your children to use the Internet for research, and you can save the money you would have otherwise spent on books and encyclopedias to provide this same information. Over the years you may find that the computer pays for itself in this respect, while opening doors for your children and helping them develop computer literacy in the process.

Island of the Lost Boys

So if you're still with us, homeschooling may be right for you. However, there are some additional considerations that may not be obvious initially. For instance, have you considered whether you can handle living like Wendy in *Peter Pan*—surrounded by only children all day long? If you have just left work to stay home with your children, this may take some getting used to. It can be very challenging, and you'll need to keep in mind your reasons for choosing this option.

It's important to remember to schedule time for grown-up interaction, too. This can be tricky, though. As it is, you may find you have a lot less time for you, so you'll have to work at carving out a little time for adult interaction. It can be done—and done successfully—if you are prepared to meet this challenge. Don't underestimate how important this time for you can be to your success as a homeschool parent.

Is Your Spouse Supportive?

Of course, spending your days surrounded by the younger set and discovering moments to carve out "you" time can be far simpler if your spouse is supportive of your homeschooling endeavor. Homeschooling success is much easier to accomplish if you have the help of a willing partner. Homeschooling is a lifestyle, and your child will learn much from both of you, even when one parent serves as the primary educator. If your spouse doubts the validity of homeschooling or criticizes your methodology (or results!) every step of the way, you will feel insecure and apprehensive, making it difficult to create the positive environment that helps homeschooled children thrive.

If your spouse is critical of homeschooling, let her read this book and any additional homeschooling literature you can provide. Let her play a role in determining how the child will be homeschooled, what subjects you will emphasize, and what methodology you will use. See our chapter "Single Parents and Working Couples" for further recommendations on how to forge a strong and united team for teaching your children.

If your spouse is still reluctant, try encouraging her to see what she can bring to the table—literally. Is your spouse a history buff? Let her be in charge of teaching history, and in this way she can share an interest with your children, while teaching them an important core subject. Or has your spouse always wanted to learn a foreign language? Suggest she do this with the children, and it can become a challenge they share. Help her recognize that this also can encourage a stronger bond with the children and help foster a stronger family bond overall. Most homeschoolers can tell you that the family that learns together, sticks together.

Do You Have What It Takes?

Homeschooling *is* an adventure, day in and day out, and is never quite what you expect. You need to be well prepared for this reality. You can plan the perfect day, and something will inevitably throw it all off. You need to be willing to stay flexible and committed. You will need to arrange your lifestyle to support homeschooling, so that even unexpected chaos, be it a doctor or dental appointment, a stopped-up toilet, or the surprise visit by your in-laws, doesn't have to interfere with your homeschooling day. This can be done by having a "homeschooling disaster preparedness plan," following some of the steps in our chapter "School on the Run."

Now that you've determined cost, impact on lifestyle, and qualifications, you need to determine whether you are ultimately up to the surprising challenges that homeschooling can bring. You won't have a regular yardstick by which to judge how you are doing. You will be responsible for encouraging yourself along the way. Additionally, realize that regardless of how popular homeschooling is today, there are still detractors—just as there are those who don't like public school or religious-based schools. You will need a level of faith in what you are doing. You need to trust that you can do this. Keep in mind that learning is a series of progressions, and like the tortoise, each small action moves you further along the road toward your goals.

Before you decide to embark on the adventure of homeschooling, consider the following:

- Are you bold and adventurous?
- Are you flexible and willing to try new things?
- Can you thrive in an environment that is organized chaos?
- If not, do you have the discipline to create a structured environment without losing your mind?
- Are you willing to venture into territories you never thought you'd explore, such as the study of amphibians or arachnids?

What Will the Neighbors Say?

We have one final caveat for you. Be prepared for the fact that regardless of how popular homeschooling has become, someone, somewhere, at some time will criticize you. Yes, there are bound to be those who talk. It may even be someone you care about, such as a parent or aunt. Then, too, there are the occasional times you will encounter a hostile interrogation by a little old lady in the grocery store who demands to know why those children aren't in school today.

The best way to deal with this is by making the case for yourself. What do we mean by this? You need to be completely convinced you are doing the right thing. Remember, you know your reasons for homeschooling. Remind yourself daily how well your children are doing, both in scholastic ability and in character development, and don't hold yourself to impossible standards. Know that your children are steadily progressing in many, many areas and that you are building an important foundation for their future success. This is what will allow criticism to roll off your back.

Don't misunderstand us, though. There will be times when this response will bother you, when you will have nagging doubts as to whether or not you are succeeding. Homeschooling is difficult in that it is hard to measure from day-to-day how well you are doing. It is only in the long run that you can see how much it has paid off. Then, when you are feeling a bit better, list all the things that you and your children have accomplished together. OK, so you fell a little behind in biology, but look how far ahead you are in history—and Susie is a polite and imaginative child! Just change gears and catch up a bit in bio, and smile to yourself. It's not a problem. And really, when it comes down to it, it really isn't any of your neighbors' business anyway.

CHAPTER 3

Single Parents and Working Couples

Historically, stay-at-home mothers have been the ones to do the home-schooling, while fathers worked long hours to support their families on single incomes. A father who did science experiments with his kids on weekends was considered to be an active participant in homeschooling. There are many couples today who would like to homeschool their children, but feel that both husband and wife should (or need to) have careers. As the homeschooling trend grows, more and more couples will be looking for ways to make homeschooling work within a dual-income family. Mothers will no longer automatically be relegated to the role of teacher, and parents may find that educating their children becomes a process in which they are both active participants. There are also a great number of single-parent families nowadays, and there are also those among this group who would like to homeschool their children as well.

How can they do this? A dual-income couple can stagger their work schedules so that at least one parent is home with the children most of the time. For most of their homeschooling years, Julie and her husband both worked full-time jobs outside of the home. She handled homeschooling Tuesdays through Fridays and then spent each weekend working 36 hours on an evening shift as a nurse in a nearby hospital. Julie's husband, Mike, worked Monday through Friday, and assumed parent and teacher duty Friday evening. Over the weekend, he'd do homeschooling activities as the need arose; for example, Julie might ask him to check over math problems, help a child proofread a story she'd written, or handle any other loose ends that needed tying up. The kids would spend Sunday evenings at their grandmother's house, taking with them work that Julie and Mike prepared for them. This gave Julie time to catch a few hours of sleep after working all night, and Mike got some treasured down time. If this sounds like a hard way to live, it is in some ways. It doesn't give parents a great deal of time one-on-one, a reality that could create big problems in some marriages. Whether or not homeschooling makes sense when both father and mother work full-time really depends upon the couple's priorities, values, personalities, needs, and a host of other factors. If both members of the couple can be reasonably content with a life where their time is largely spent either at the workplace or engaged with kids, they can be successful— especially if the parents commit to making time for their relationship, even if it's only minimal.

Perhaps another homeschooling parent in your area would be willing to incorporate your child's schoolwork into their homeschooling day in order to earn some extra income. Obviously, you'd need to know the person well enough to be comfortable with how they will handle your child's schoolwork. If both parents will be working full-time, they will have to pare down their usual activities to make time for homeschooling. If they have already been sharing the child care duties, much of the scheduling is already in place; but they will have to find a way to make time for homeschooling each week. It doesn't require as much time as one might think. Depending on whom you ask, parents need to allow somewhere between one and four hours per day for homeschooling. Very young children may only need an hour or two, whereas older ones may require more time. However, the parent can often do other things for a few minutes throughout the time that a child is working on something independently. Plus, there should be time for field trips, visits to libraries, and the like. Dual-income couples that homeschool have very busy lives, but can make homeschooling work if they're able to make the commitment.

Defining Your Shared Goals

Coordinating your efforts will take some planning, clear communication, and willingness to negotiate compromises with your spouse if you have major differences in your visions of what homeschooling life should be like. Many homeschooling parents have definite ideas about the education of children in general, and if you discover that you and your spouse have vastly different notions of your system of homeschooling, you will probably head off a lot of future frustration and conflict if you make a real effort to work together to come up with a goal you can agree upon. It's hard to accomplish anything if team members don't have a shared goal. Imagine a soccer game in which the teams are fairly evenly matched. Sometimes the ball gets kicked through the goalpost at one end of the field, and other times it gets kicked through the goalpost at the opposite end of the field. Both teams do a great job at protecting their goal most of the time. This is a clear case of competition, each moving the ball toward the other's goal, each protecting their own goal. Do you want to be competing with your partner toward achieving oppositional goals or working toward a common one? Of course, you want to work toward a common goal!

Now, imagine the rules of our soccer game have changed. Suppose both soccer teams suddenly decided that instead of trying to win the game, they'd rather work together to get the ball to the 50 yard line? How difficult would that be? It would be far simpler. No one would be standing in your way, and in fact, you'd have twice as many people assisting you in achieving your goal. While this is unrealistic in a soccer game, you can see how this analogy demonstrates that a change in paradigm can make it far simpler to achieve your homeschooling goals. Your spouse *is* your partner. Identify what you are working toward, and set the plan in motion.

Homeschooling will be far more relaxing, comfortable, and efficient if you and your spouse band together and define your mutual mission. Since homeschooling is a lifestyle in which parenting and teaching typically become intertwined, it is hard to distinguish one from the other. So it pays to look at your parenting goals at the same time you are looking at your educational goals.

Sometimes a couple can have widely divergent views that threaten to cause serious conflict, and this may make them think homeschooling is impossible. Even if one of you believes that your homeschool should be run with the discipline and structure found in the military, while your spouse unequivocally embraces the unschooling approach that dismisses formal structure, you may find you can make homeschooling work if you both want to find a way. Set your sights on finding a win-win situation. Yes, on the surface, it may seem that compromise isn't possible. Each of you has deeply held beliefs that you feel you need to honor. So, what next? In these sorts of situations, each member of a couple often jumps to conclusions about what it is the other person is proposing. Figure out and share with your spouse the specific goal that you feel requires homeschooling/parenting your way. Define your goals for homeschooling and have your spouse define his. There are probably some that you haven't really discussed with one another. You may find you have different goals, but that they can be combined well. For instance, the parent who wishes to educate with a militarylike precision might have the following goal: "develop self-discipline, the ability to do a job well, and complete it in a timely manner," while the other parent's goal may be: "acquire academic skills and knowledge to help ensure the child's ability to make a living." The "difference" may be a matter of focus. You likely each want what your partner wants, but it just hasn't been your primary focus. So, you must stop and ask yourself, do you really want different things, or do you want the same things, although you prioritize or focus on different aspects of the same thing?

No matter which homeschooling approach you take, getting together with your spouse to do some planning before your homeschool year begins will help you get off to a smoother start. If you hope to achieve an equal partnership in your homeschooling effort, you must devise a plan for the year rather than having one of the partners make all the decisions. This way each parent is participating, rather than just assisting in the implementation of the other's ideas. If one of you works far more hours than the other, it may seem natural for the spouse who is at home with the kids more often to take over more of the decision making. However, this may not be a good idea. If both parents remain fully involved, mom and dad will both feel some accountability for the results. That way, when Johnny can't read on schedule, neither partner is left shouldering all the blame. Instead of mom worrying how to solve this problem alone, she can discuss the problem with her partner, and together they can work to figure out a solution. Another good reason to have dad involved is because it avoids having a little boy coming to believe that school is "a girl thing." Dad's involvement demonstrates that males love learning, parenting, and teaching, as well. Additionally, it serves as a model for embracing many roles in life, not just ones traditionally defined for us by society at large.

Planning

Once you've established your goals, you need to work together to develop a plan to make them happen. For unschoolers, planning could be simply a matter of deciding who will take the kids on trips to the library, or the dance studio, and which books, kits, and craft or hobby materials you plan to buy for kids with particular interests. Parents who favor the more structured school at home approach may lay out a detailed plan for the year. They will need to decide which textbooks and other educational supplies to use, who is going to learn what and when, and who will teach the various subjects.

You may decide to set specific goals pertaining to academic achievement for the coming year so that you can reach your larger overall education goals. Clarity in definition of your goals for the school year will go a long way toward helping you accomplish all your goals. Additionally, it is a good way to make sure you both are in agreement as to what is covered and how homeschooling will be implemented in your household.

Once you've discussed annual goals, you need to determine your particular curriculum, as well as any other materials you may want to use. From there, figure out how this will fit into your day. Develop a routine you can both be comfortable with—even if it is a matter of having little routine and lots of spontaneous activities. The most important goal is to become unified in your purposes. Finally, make sure you know who will be doing what and when. This will help avoid any conflicts from a lack of understanding about who is accountable for what. Once you've done this, leave it to your partner to do his thing successfully, while you do your own part.

Homeschooling and the Single Parent

The single parent who must work to earn a living but feels her child would be best served by homeschooling, will have to have help with child care and possibly with the teaching. If the parent can arrange child care and work during the evenings, from 3 p.m. to 11 p.m., or on weekends, she could be free to homeschool her child each morning. A couple of hours of solid homeschooling can accomplish quite a lot. The parent could spend this time teaching the subjects that require her presence, such as a new math topic, and while the parent is at work, leave items that the child can do independently or can work on under the supervision of her sitter.

Another option is that of single parents joining together to homeschool their children as a team, though not all states have homeschooling laws that allow a two-family homeschooling arrangement. They would have to maintain work schedules that accommodate this arrangement. On days that one parent works, the other can take care of all the children, teaching them as a group, and vice versa. This system can work well if both parents have similar goals and teaching styles. This can be a great solution; however, if the two parents can't agree on how homeschooling ought to be conducted, there is great potential for conflict. A parent must choose their education partner carefully, since that partner will be spending so much time with their child. On the other hand, if the parents are too rigid in their requirements, they will be less likely to find a suitable partner.

Laura found this to be a terrific way to homeschool her children in tandem with her friend Janine. However, it took a lot of effort on their part to make it work. They realized immediately the need for a highly structured system, in which all potential pitfalls were addressed beforehand. They included not just educational structure, but parenting structure as well. Both moms realized that disciplinary action would have to be defined for any offense, be it not completing assignments or stealing cookies from the cookie jar. This was the only way to avoid accusations of favoritism, which the children would initially attempt to play upon.

After an initial period in which the children predictably tested the rules, things began to run smoothly. Together they ran their individual households and homeschool programs as if they were one. Not only are the children successfully cared for and educated, but the experience has enriched the lives of both families.

If you are a single parent interested in homeschooling, you may not know where to begin to look for a partner. If you don't happen to have a suitable homeschooling acquaintance, a good place to start would be homeschooling groups. Contact a state homeschooling organization (see Appendix B) and obtain information about homeschooling support groups in your area. You could call group leaders and ask whether they know a single parent who may be interested in teaming up with another one, or you could attend a few meetings, ask around, and see if anyone you meet knows of someone who might be worth contacting. You could post messages on homeschooling message boards online or place an ad in a local newspaper. Obviously, you want to be careful to make sure your child will be safe with whomever you team up with, so use some common sense in evaluating the other parent. It's wise to visit each other in your homes a few times, make sure the family's environment is a safe and healthy one for your child, and determine whether there are any other people living there or visiting that would be in contact with your child, and if so, whether you are comfortable with them. You might exchange personal references and even arrange for background checks of each other.

If you are considering teaming up with another homeschooling parent, here are some basic questions you need to ask each other before you decide to take that step. This way you can negotiate compromises if necessary, or find out in advance if your venture is doomed to fail because of vast differences in parenting or educational philosophies.

- Why do you want to homeschool your child, and what benefits do you want him to gain from it?
- How do you define a good education?
- Are there any subjects you would like to give more attention to than conventional schools do? Or less attention? If so, why?

Checking In

If you and your partner have clarified your goals and developed an education plan, you are nearly ready to get started. One last suggestion, though, is that you devise some organized method by which to check in with one another, so that you will each be kept abreast of important information pertaining to your child's progress and other aspects of day-to-day homeschooling issues. It may be helpful to establish a routine whereby a parent who is turning over homeschooling to the other parent for the afternoon, day, or other period of time passes on information to the parent who is about to take over. If you don't do it with face-to-face conversation, you might leave notes for each other in a designated place, send each other e-mails, or use whatever form of communication works best for you and your partner. Julie uses a handy mnemonic device, USE PS, to help remember things she needs to pass along to her spouse, Mike, before she goes to work. Here's how it works.

U stands for Unfinished business. This is anything that Mike needs to follow through on: "Martin's math problems still need to be checked," or "Today is the last day for Madeleine to enroll in dance for this year."

S stands for Supplies. This refers to books and other school resources: "Isabel finished Volume 1 of her math workbook. I think Volume 2 is on the top shelf of the hall closet under a pile of papers."

E stands for Equipment. This could relate to computers, your automobile, or other things that, when malfunctioning, can interfere with your homeschooling that day: "A lightning strike destroyed the modem, so I'm taking the computer to the shop today."

P stands for Problems. This means issues having to do with the child herself: "Isabel got frustrated and started crying today while she was studying spelling words. She said spelling is boring, and she hates it."

S stands for Suggestions. This is for your input on dealing with a problem you mentioned or simply a new idea you would like to share with your partner: "Maybe Isabel would rather learn spelling by playing a computer spelling game. We could look and see what CD Roms are available," or "Madeleine wants to learn how to build a Web page using HTML. Maybe you and she can find some resources today to help her get started."

You can follow these guidelines, or come up with whatever method is practical in your situation. Just make sure that, one way or another, you keep each other informed.

- Are there any topics that you would avoid teaching your child because they clash with your religious or philosophical beliefs?

- What are your methods of correcting inappropriate behaviors in children?

- What is your definition of a well-behaved child?

- How do you feel about another adult correcting your child, and is it important that it be done in the same way you do it?

- What child behaviors do you find most intolerable?

- How much structure do you think will work best for your home-schooled child, for example, unstructured unschooling or highly structured approach?

These are very probing questions that should give you a fairly clear idea of what sort of homeschooling partner the other parent will make. Keep in mind that you probably won't find a homeschooling partner with whom you share precisely the same views on every issue. Figure out areas where you can make compromises without feeling as if you're a bad parent, and be clear about which ones aren't negotiable.

Clarifying Your Vision

One great thing about homeschooling is the wide variety of choices it provides. The novice homeschoolers may find this exhilarating or intimidating. Regardless of how you feel about this, there are decisions you will have to make. What these decisions ultimately are will depend a lot on both your personality and your philosophy on education. This philosophy may be well developed if you have been pondering homeschooling for years, or the notion of educating your child yourself may be so new to you that you aren't sure what the various schools of homeschooling are about, much less which is right for you.

To give you an idea as to how diverse the methodology of homeschooling is, understand that there are veteran homeschoolers who believe that children do best in an unstructured learning situation and others who believe a homeschool should be run like a well-oiled machine, with everything being taught according to a predetermined plan. The latter tend to focus on discipline of habit as the key to responsibility and education, while the former tend to see pursuing learning solely for the love of learning as the key. The more relaxed homeschoolers believe it is wrong to push a child to learn something he or she doesn't want to learn. These "unschoolers" have faith that their child's natural curiosity, coupled with their desire to participate in the adult world, will ensure that the child will eventually learn everything he or she needs to know.

Between these two poles are countless blends of beliefs about how much educational freedom children should have.

Just as each of us may have a unique perspective on homeschooling approaches, each of our children has a unique blend of personality traits, interests, talents, strengths, and weaknesses. This can influence the approach the parent chooses as well, as they hash out the details of methodology, subject matter, areas of emphasis, schedules, and mandatory requirements. Over the years, our own approaches to homeschooling have evolved steadily and at times have undergone radical changes, until we found the balance that works for us. You may find this to be the case in your homeschool as well.

In this chapter we will briefly describe to you the different approaches homeschoolers commonly use, so that you can get an idea of how to structure (or not) your day. Try what seems most logical to you, and then adjust accordingly as you go along. In short order you should choose the style that works best for your family. It may be one that adheres to a specific school of thought, or it may be a combination of several. The most important thing is to do what works for you and for your children. Each family is unique, and that is part of what makes homeschooling so exciting—the ability to embrace your uniqueness and create a method tailor-made for you!

Highly Structured

The image that comes to mind for many when they think of homeschooling is that of children seated around a table doing work in their textbooks. This is a very "school at home" approach, in which the classroom setting is re-created in the home. Is this how you see your day?

Are you the sort of person who is ultraorganized, feeling more comfortable when you have every minute of every day mapped out in detail, weeks in advance? Do your children thrive in this kind of environment? If so, you may be most comfortable if you use a highly structured approach to homeschooling.

You might find that your key to success is found in planning your curriculum by setting goals for each child: overall ones, quarterly ones, and daily ones. You can simplify planning by purchasing one of the prepackaged curricula and following the premade plan, having your child complete the required work each day.

If you would rather be more involved, you can opt to design your own curriculum. If you choose this path, you will probably want to find out which topics and skills are traditionally taught in each grade to help you plan. Sometimes you can get this information from the local public school system, but you can find this information in books from the local library. E. D. Hirsch's *What Your _____ Grader Needs to Know* (Delta) series suggests what to teach at each of the grade levels, but his recommendations are more advanced than what is taught in many schools. Additionally, we have included a typical scope and sequence of study in the back of this book.

Consider planning your lessons far enough in advance to allow time for you to get any library books or supplies you may need. Keep in mind that while you have a very organized educational plan, life still happens. You'll need to have a plan for days when the unexpected occurs, for example, Suzie falls out of a tree and needs stitches, or you have to spend the morning getting a car repaired. You could simply build an extra number of days into the school year so that you may cancel school when such crises arrive, or find some other way to cope. You will find other options for dealing with such situations in our "School on the Run" chapter; however, you will find it more difficult to stray from your typical program of study if you must complete a prepackaged curricula or work with a school-at-home program that requires your child to complete and turn in work at a set time. Keep this in mind when you consider this option. Regardless of that caveat, you may find that you are the type of family that thrives when following this approach to homeschooling. Read on, though, to get an idea of other methods you can consider.

Unschooling

You may be the type of person who hates the idea of planning out every minute of your child's time. For you, "unschooling" may be the more appropriate approach to your homeschooling lifestyle.

You can determine this by asking yourself a few questions: Are you comfortable with a more laissez-faire approach to life? If Johnny isn't yet interested in learning to read by the time first grade rolls around, will you fly into a panic? Or will you just shrug your shoulders and decide he must just not be ready yet?

Unschooling parents believe you optimize children's natural learning desires if you allow them to follow their own inclinations. They trust that children's innate sense of curiosity will ensure that they eventually learn everything they need to know. While many would feel uncomfortable with this format, there are others who believe this is the whole point of choosing homeschooling.

Typically, unschooling parents function as facilitators for learning, rather than as teachers. The parent helps the child find the proper resources to learn what he wants to learn. For example, if Joey wants to learn about frogs, Joey's mom may take him to the library and help him find books on frogs. She may even take Joey to a creek to catch a frog or help him find additional materials, as well as reading to the child from higher-level books on the topic and answering questions on the subject at hand.

Unschooling parents may even discover that they spend an inordinate amount of time learning about frogs, but this is okay, since they have no preset curriculum to adhere to, and Joey is certainly learning and has maintained his passion for knowledge, keeping his sense of curiosity intact.

Unit Studies

While you have those who re-create school at home, and those who reject anything "school-ish" whatsoever, there are others who prefer a level of structure, but also wish to allow their children to follow their curiosity in determining the subjects to study. Unit studies take all or most of the school subjects and roll them into a cohesive unit centered around one topic of study.

For instance, if you are studying the Atlantic Ocean, spelling words can be ocean related, reading can be a study of sea life, science can include learning about mammals of the sea, music can be learning a sea chanty, art can include drawing sea mammals, social studies can be the study of pirates and trade routes, and if you get creative you can probably find a way to work math into the unit, though many parents opt to teach math separately. You might even help them prepare a seafood meal for dinner and incorporate a trip to a local aquarium.

You can put a lot of time and effort into planning a unit study, or you can teach quickie mini-units. If a child shows an interest in gardening, for instance, you might pick up some books from the library and read about plant structure together or read about cross-pollination. When you and the child begin tilling the soil and planting seeds, you can talk about what you read. You can end your unit there, satisfied that your child has learned a nice bit about gardening and understands some biology about it. However, you *could* opt to go further, perhaps noting the number of seeds you planted and charting the rate at which they grow. You may want to plant some in full sun, some in partial sun, and some in shade. Then you may track their growth and graph the results. You could go further still and determine the statistical rate of survival of these seeds when in full sun, partial sun, and shade. Do you see how units can grow?

You can then take this across the curriculum and perhaps study the history of farming or what role certain crops played during certain periods of history. The seeds in the garden will then be not just a lesson on their own, but the springboard to a whole variety of lessons across the curriculum, all tied together by the common thread of your garden.

How do you choose a topic for a unit study? You can define a unit study based on your child's personal interests, such as in the examples above, or you can intentionally create unit studies when you plan your curriculum for the year. Perhaps you are a homeschooler who prefers a highly structured curriculum. You may choose themes for the year or for each season. The more relaxed homeschooler may prefer to choose themes that seem to evolve from things. Both ways work, so just approach unit studies in whatever way is most comfortable for you.

Eclectic

Perhaps there are aspects of each method that you find appealing. Terrific! This isn't a bad thing. Say you like the idea of letting a child learn things she's interested in, but you're a little skeptical of unschooling.

Creating Unit Studies

Creating your own unit studies isn't very difficult. Below we take you through the steps to create a unit study of your own. Don't be intimidated by the number of steps. We've broken it down into the smallest pieces possible so that you can better understand how to structure one, but it really isn't that hard, especially if you stick to topics you are all fascinated with! So, to begin, follow these steps.

1. Determine your topic. You can either choose a topic yourself or go with a topic your children are intrigued with. However, you *do* need to determine for yourself *why* you feel this topic deserves a unit dedicated to it. Is it because your kids are interested in it, and you've never studied it before? Is it because you find the feudal system fascinating and feel the Middle Ages would make a great unit study, into which you can incorporate knights and castles? Is it because it is on a standard scope and sequence you studied? Or perhaps you saw a question alluding to it in a practice standardized test and panicked upon realizing you've never covered that topic. Really, the reason behind your choice doesn't matter. What matters is *knowing* the reason, as this will help you determine how you approach the topic.

2. Determine whether you want to study the topic in-depth or simply introduce it to your children . . . *before* you plan your unit!

3. Determine how much knowledge your children already have on the topic. You should include this aspect so that you won't discover you've planned some introductory activities that were unnecessary.

4. Determine your objectives. If you are studying a time period, such as the Middle Ages, what exactly are you aiming to study? Life at the time? Famous people of the period? Economic structure? Political climate? Inventions of the period? Historical events? You need to do this to limit your scope, *especially* when approaching a broad topic.

5. Look on the Internet for resources that may be useful.

6. Look to resources you may have at home, such as encyclopedias or history or other reference books.

7. Visit your library to find books on the topic.

8. Visit local museums that have exhibits on your topic, or explore other community outreach programs. Your local community exten-

(continued on page 35)

(continued from page 34)

sion office may have materials that can support a science unit study, for instance.

9. Determine how long you will spend on the unit: two weeks, a month, six weeks.

10. Draw pictures of your spelling and vocabulary words when it is applicable, such as when your unit covers dolphins, penguins, and so on.

11. Explore any art projects you could do to reinforce the activity, be it coloring pages, collages, or dioramas. Art projects usually help reinforce the topic in a fun way!

12. Determine if you want to do additional supplemental activities. Do you want to create a timeline for this period? Perhaps map work needs to be done?

13. Determine what kind of writing assignment could be used in this unit. Could your children keep a creative journal, pretending they lived during the time period or event you are studying? Are they perhaps an astronaut on the first manned space flight, if you are doing a space unit? They could write a creative piece on the experience, from the point of view of the astronaut, or keep a journal of what astronaut training was like. Perhaps there is a form of writing that is particular to the topic being studied? Maybe you could write limericks, or haikus, or another specialized form of writing related to the topic? Get creative, and make the writing aspect as much fun as you possibly can!

14. Some like to incorporate math into the unit study and sometimes this can be done, though you may well find that this doesn't provide a strong enough math curricula. So you may opt to simply add neat little math tidbits that tie into your unit when appropriate, yet maintain a separate math curricula entirely.

15. Break it down. Look over the scope and breadth of the material you hope to cover and the projects you are incorporating to support it. How much time do you expect each will take? Plot it out on your calendar.

16. Stay flexible! If you find that one aspect becomes stressful or boring for everyone, feel free to adjust the course as necessary! As long as you keep your objective in mind, you won't stray far and will accomplish *tons* while still having a great time!

Many homeschooling parents take an eclectic approach, combining what they feel is the best of the different styles. They may insist that a child do a certain amount of math each day, while allowing her freedom to study whichever science topic interests her at the moment. This homeschool parent might have most of the child's schoolwork planned out and highly structured, while leaving some room to accommodate the child's preferences.

For instance, Laura uses Saxon math with Brandon and Chris, but allows them to choose from a wide variety of preapproved literature for reading. Additionally, she uses different math drill methods to further support what they learn in Saxon. Laura finds that the hodge-podge of educational materials they use allows her family to explore fully all the wonderful options out there, instead of locking them into one particular curriculum. In this way, they feel able to use the crème de la crème of homeschooling/educational products, while giving the children a more rounded education. However, it does take some effort to ensure you aren't missing something important along the way. With a good scope and sequence in hand, though, this isn't very difficult to do.

You may find that using this method leaves you open to a lot of trial and error, as well. You may try four different grammar products before you hit upon the one your children are most responsive to. However, at least you have the freedom to try other approaches, something we found we couldn't do when following one prescribed fully structured curriculum. Laura's family enjoyed this element of flexibility and found that it also left open the opportunity to try approaches such as unit studies when they found a topic to be exceptionally inspirational.

CHAPTER 5

Taking the Plunge

IN THIS CHAPTER

✔ Defining attendance

✔ Lesson plans

✔ Transition and deschooling

You're really going to do it. You've figured out how to handle the cost, the juggling of schedules, talked with homeschoolers in your area, and informed the kids. You've also clarified your vision of what you hope to accomplish—and you've determined which methodology you wish to try. Congratulations, you're ready to take the plunge.

Now you need to get legal. You have to determine if, where, and how to register as a homeschooler. You're ready to figure out how you can get down to the nuts and bolts of mandatory record keeping, lesson planning, and any other requirements of your state.

This chapter will help you figure out where to begin. Hang tough—this isn't as complicated as it sounds, and you will see that it can be done fairly easily.

While homeschooling is legal in every state, the ways in which the various states regulate homeschooling range from hands off to highly restrictive. In Alaska, for instance, in order to homeschool a child the parents can simply begin homeschooling, one of several options for establishing a homeschool there. They are not required to possess any qualifications in order to teach, to teach any particular subjects, to keep any sort of records, or even to notify their state or local school authorities of their intention to educate their children at home. Homeschoolers in North Dakota, on the other hand, are subject to numerous requirements. Their state law specifies which subjects must be taught and how many days and hours must be devoted to schooling. It also mandates record keeping and standardized testing. Furthermore, in North Dakota, a homeschooling parent without a bachelor's degree must homeschool under the supervision of a certified teacher for at least two years, unless he or she passes the National Teacher Exam.

If you live in a state like North Dakota, you may wonder if all those regulations make homeschooling impractical for you. The prospect of having your homeschool program supervised by a traditional teacher may be repugnant to you, or at the very least, intimidating, especially if you believe an unstructured unschooling approach would be the best way for your kids to learn. Don't despair, though. Complying with your state's homeschooling regulations may not be as difficult or as limiting as they first seem. There are often creative ways to comply with the law without giving up so much of your freedom to educate your children as you see fit. This sort of information is often best garnered by asking veteran homeschooling parents how they comply with the laws while maintaining as much autonomy as possible. You'll find state home-schooling support groups listed in Appendix B of this book. Additionally, most states have local community homeschooling support groups as well. Talking to a homeschooling support group leader and visiting support group meetings before you begin homeschooling are good ways to learn the ins and outs of complying with state regulations. For example, perhaps the group knows of certified teachers who are home-schooling friendly and will supervise a homeschooling program without intimidating you or telling you how to run the show. Further, they can likely tell you the simplest ways to keep records to satisfy state requirements.

Defining Attendance

When it comes to record keeping, attendance seems most often required by states. Compulsory attendance laws vary from state to state, so in order to determine what your legal requirements are at this time, refer to Appendix A in this book. Additionally, we recommend you contact your state homeschool agency to ensure the requirements haven't changed. Further, ask a local support group member how the law is interpreted and enforced in your area, as again this varies from place to place and sometimes from community to community.

We recommend you keep an attendance sheet, even if your state doesn't require it, just in case you are ever questioned regarding attendance in your homeschool. You can do this by using a simple form that you purchase from a homeschool supply store, a calendar that you maintain for this purpose, or a state-provided form.

There are some things you may want to consider when planning your school schedule and how to log attendance. If your state doesn't have laws that specify the days/dates when you must school (and most do not), you may find you have an enormous amount of flexibility. You can opt to school six days a week, or through the summers, or four days one week, six days the next, as long as you ensure that you school for at least the minimum days required.

You may want to maintain some kind of structure to your schedule, developing a routine so that your children can know what to expect and when. However, it can be a loose structure, if you'd prefer. Simply understand how your schedule will work, and you will find that you have time, and opportunity, to take advantage of things most families cannot squeeze into their busy lives.

Is your son anxiously awaiting the opening of the phenomenal new dinosaur exhibit at a nearby science museum? You learn it opens on a Tuesday at 2 p.m. when you typically do art class. Well, guess what? You can reschedule art and take advantage of the exhibit opening, which may well be less crowded since most children are in school at that time.

How does this apply to attendance? A trip to the museum solely for enjoyment is *not* missed school time. This is a science field trip, and you need to make sure to count it as such when you are documenting attendance. If you are anything like the typical homeschooling family, you will discover that so much of what you do and how you interact with your children actually *is* a learning experience. If you begin paying attention to such nuances, even die-hard unschoolers will find they never have trouble meeting—or logging—minimum attendance requirements.

Think of all those talks in the car, from conversations about where fuel comes from to why the sky appears blue—those are all educational, aren't they? Make sure you give yourself credit for such things. As long as you are doing the important basics at home, these bonus opportunities for learning serve to further enhance your child's education and you have every right to take credit for it.

Now, this doesn't mean you can hit the beach and call it school. However, read a book on seashells and ocean life, go to the beach to collect shells to study, and later compare them to what you found in the book and enjoy some sun and fun in the process. You can then make crafts with the shells at home in the evening and talk of ocean life, and you can give yourself some credit for science, art, and gym. Evaluate the time you spent on educational activities fairly, and log it if you truly did teach that day. Remember, fair evaluation also means giving credit where credit is due!

The process of logging educational time can get complicated, because so many homeschoolers find that life itself is a continuing education. Supermarket trips, doctor's visits, and taking the car for an oil change all become learning experiences in the homeschool world. Just make sure you evaluate your time fairly in both directions. You're likely to discover that your children spend far more time engrossed in learning than required by compulsory attendance laws.

Lesson Plans

Some states require records of actual lesson plans, and some parents find a sense of comfort in having those plans, whereas others dread this level of structure, feeling it prevents them from embracing opportunities that spring up out of the blue. So, approaches to lesson planning will vary from one homeschool to another. A homeschooler's personal preference and methodology will affect how he or she approaches lesson planning. An unschooler will not really have lesson plans, or at least is more likely to have informal ones. If they must present lesson plans, some do so by journaling what they do each day, while others turn in more of a skeleton plan that can be interpreted—and applied—quite flexibly. If you are an unschooler who lives in a state where you need to file lesson plans, your best bet is to find other unschoolers in your area and learn how they handle this specific requirement.

A homeschooling family that uses a complete prepackaged curriculum such as A-Beka or Calvert won't have much lesson planning to do, as the lessons come preplanned. However, depending on the program you use, there may be some work required to prepare for the lesson, such as getting supplies together or getting a particular book from the library. Families that take the eclectic approach may find that they feel better planning out a highly structured daily curriculum from which they rarely deviate so as to incorporate the curriculum into their routine—or they may find that they prefer to have a looser structure around which to create their homeschooling day.

Since families using full prepackaged curricula don't typically have to address lesson planning, and as unschoolers opt not to plan lessons, we are going to focus on the eclectic and unit-study approaches.

If you're worried about missing something important when homeschooling your child, it may ease your mind to follow the scope and sequence found in Appendix E to get a general idea of what you need to cover as you create your lesson plans. Once you determine what you want to teach, you need to plan out how and when.

What makes for a good lesson plan? A good plan helps you achieve your overall goals by moving you toward them one step at a time. To create your plan, begin by examining what it is you hope to accomplish in the upcoming year. From there, determine *how* you will teach those subjects. Have you chosen a math curriculum that you like? How about language arts? What are you going to do for writing this year? Consider each subject area, and determine whether or not you plan on using unit studies and, if so, how you will incorporate them into your school year.

Will you do a unit study each month? Will you use a unit study to teach across the curriculum or just to address a particular subject area, such as science or history? If you determine that unit studies will be merely supplemental material, how will you fit them in? During unit studies, will you suspend normal activities in that subject area? Will you do them only on Saturdays perhaps?

Or have you decided you wish to incorporate unit studies across the curriculum? If that is the case, will you temporarily suspend your other curriculum when doing a unit study? These are lesson-planning decisions you will want to address before determining your weekly and daily lesson planning breakdowns.

Once you've made all these decisions, it's time to get down to planning! Begin by determining what you want to cover in each subject area this year. Set specific goals for the 3 Rs, science, social studies, art, language, physical education, and any additional subjects you hope to cover.

From there, break your goals down into specific segments. Is your writing goal to teach your children to write a great fictional story? Perhaps first you will work on studying good fiction (reading class) and analyzing the structure. Next you will want to study theme development. Then plot the action. You will also have to cover topics such as main characters and foreshadowing, depending upon your children's previous knowledge. Next you will want to have them begin writing an outline and later to flesh out the story. Then there will be edits and rewrites as you help them better grasp all the important nuances of putting together a well-written story.

So, you now have a list of tasks that need to be accomplished. Next, organize it according to your time schedule. When will you have your children do each of these things? Log it in, and voilà, you have a lesson plan. Continue to do this for each subject area, and soon your job will be done. All that's left to do is follow it.

Transition and Deschooling

Once you've decided how you will integrate homeschooling into your life, set your school goals, and create lesson plans, you will have to look at even more practical matters—how you will handle the first days of homeschooling. If your children have been attending a traditional school, you need to consider how they will respond to being pulled from school. Many children are happy at first, for a variety of reasons. Be forewarned, your children may believe they are going to have an easy time of it—or conversely, that their life will be more difficult than ever before. You may feel pressured to set the record straight from the very beginning.

This isn't a bad idea, and having a discussion of what you will expect from your children prior to initiating homeschooling is a good idea.

Additionally, when you actually pull your children from school, you may find that you don't want to leap right into homeschooling the very next day.

Many homeschooling experts believe that the transition from traditional school to homeschooling should incorporate a period of what is commonly referred to as *deschooling*. Deschooling is simply a period in which you allow your children to take a break and adapt to this new sense of freedom, so that they can be better prepared to experience a different kind of schooling than what they are accustomed to.

Why is this necessary? Keep in mind that even if you choose a highly structured approach to schooling, your children's school day will be vastly different than what they are accustomed to. They will have a new routine to get used to and a schedule that will need to be learned and followed. Also, they will have to adapt to living and working in the same place—something some self-employed adults even struggle with.

Your children will likely test their limits in this new setting, too. How strict will mom or dad be? How much can they get away with? Can they now play video games and watch television at times when other children are going to school? Your child *is* experiencing a newfound sense of freedom, one that can be both exhilarating and frightening. There may also be apprehension toward the unknown factors—yeah, homeschooling *sounds* great, but will it really be great? Parent and child are probably both wondering this, as well as questioning if this will really work.

These mixed emotions are not unusual. Many children initially see the early days of homeschooling as they would see summer vacation—school's out! It is also common for parents to assert quickly that they mean business when it comes to schooling, fearing that their child won't take them seriously otherwise.

However, if you allow your child to deschool before beginning your school program, you might reduce much of this, as many children actually get bored when they have too much time on their hands. Think of how eager many children are to return to school after a long summer break. Furthermore, this can provide a great springboard into a new approach to learning.

Laura found that when she pulled Brandon out of a multiage public school program midyear in order to begin homeschooling, she had to let him deschool. In their case, Brandon was excited at the idea of homeschooling, but wasn't sure what to expect. Laura announced that they would take a four-week break from work before homeschooling would commence; however, during normal school hours there would be no television or video games. So while Laura gave Brandon pretty much free rein over his time, she made sure he wouldn't be frittering it on television and games. These two simple restrictions worked like a charm. Brandon found he needed to get creative in order to enjoy himself for that many hours in a day. Yes, Brandon did spend time playing with action figures and legos; however, he also took long nature walks with Laura and Chris, studying the habitats of local woodland animals and learning about different insects. He also spent a lot of time drawing, painting, reading, and writing stories. Laura also took him on trips to local museums, the library, and to local government buildings. Brandon was also allowed (and encouraged) to play educational games on the computer.

The end result was that Brandon actually learned quite a bit during those four weeks. However, the learning occurred in a very unschooling way. Brandon felt he was getting away with not having to do schoolwork, but actually expanded his repertoire of knowledge a great deal, having fun in the process. This served to remind him that learning new things could be exciting and not just a chore—something he had begun to feel when he was attending public school.

This experience gave Brandon a taste of what homeschooling would be like, while allowing him to adapt to a more relaxed approach to education. At the end of the four weeks, Laura continued to approach many school subjects in the same manner, but added formal reading, writing, and math lessons to their daily routine, ultimately creating an eclectic homeschool lifestyle that has continued to work for her family.

CHAPTER 6

Standardized Testing

IN THIS CHAPTER

✔ When your children score poorly

✔ Which test?

✔ What to do with the results

✔ Preparing your children for testing

✔ Some sources for standardized tests

There is one final area of legal compliance you may have to face, although it is an aspect that some parents find stressful. While it may not be the case where you live, standardized testing is a fact of life for many homeschoolers. Currently, about 30 states have laws that require standardized testing or some other type of evaluation of homeschooled children's progress. Some homeschoolers embrace this opportunity, while others, if they are not required to administer an exam, will never give much thought to the standardized testing of their homeschooled children until college plans are being considered and their children need to pass SATs and other entrance exams.

For parents who are not required to administer a standardized test, the decision of whether to do so is anything but simple. Many people have strong opinions about standardized testing, and for those examining the pros and cons of administering them when it is not required, the issue can be befuddling.

If you grew up seeing standardized tests as a normal part of life, you may not have given this much thought, especially if you tended to do well on them. Standardized tests can certainly provide validation when your children score well and can give you just the boost you need when you are struggling to determine if your homeschooling efforts are truly paying off. This may well be the only *concrete* yardstick by which you can measure your children's progress. Yes, you may believe your children are doing well, and you can see the wonderful qualities they exhibit—all things which indicate they are growing up into intelligent and confident young people. However, when relatives or friends comment on your methods, or ask how you know you aren't "ruining your children," a drawer filled with annual test results can be reassuring—and can also be whipped out to satisfy even the nosiest people, if you feel the need to prove yourself (we hope you don't feel that need, though!).

Standardized tests can also serve to illustrate whether your children have kept pace with their traditionally schooled counterparts. Julie learned from a standardized test that one of her children didn't understand the purpose of a zip code. This same child could write and address letters and was very advanced in other subject areas, but lost points for not knowing why zip codes exist. Julie was able to correct this with a simple explanation. While she likely would have eventually caught this without the test, the test did serve to bring this missed piece of information to her attention.

As you can see, test results can provide comfort to a homeschooler who is looking for feedback on how their program is going. On the other hand, test results can also be frightening. Your children may score very poorly, even though you *know* they are extremely bright and perhaps even academically gifted. Why, then, would they score poorly?

There are a variety of reasons, and this is why some parents abhor standardized tests. They feel that the tests are designed to be suited to only one style of learner—if your child is a kinesthetic learner who cannot sit still for a long test, she may do poorly on an exam, even though she is very bright. Or if your child isn't feeling well on test day, the results can be skewed. Or, although you may have covered a wide variety of topics, in fact, far more than your child may have covered in a traditional school setting, the topics didn't correlate with the topics covered in the exam, and subsequently your child scores poorly. Laura's boys have a very advanced understanding of genetics, for instance (inspired by a fascination with the X-men cartoon that led to their studying extremely advanced information). However, even though their understanding of genetics exceeds that of a high school student, their knowledge of biology placed them only at their current grade level on the standardized test.

If you have an option to test or not to test, determine what it is that you want to gain from the exam. If you are simply looking for bragging rights, you may be testing for the wrong reason. However, if you are trying to follow a standard scope and sequence, and therefore likely to have covered the topics on the exam during the academic year, you may enjoy using a standardized test to reassure you that your children are progressing properly. However, bear in mind that if they score poorly, there could be a number of reasons, and be sure you take that into consideration before assuming you are failing at homeschooling.

When Your Children Score Poorly

If your children do poorly in one or more areas on the exam, you will want to look at the circumstances to better understand what is going on. Were your children inexperienced with the testing format, and therefore overwhelmed by the test itself? If so, you may want to evaluate their abilities in another way, such as by asking them oral questions. Before the next exam, you may want to have them take some practice exams so that they are better prepared to face a testing situation.

Perhaps you failed to cover a topic addressed on the exam? If so, don't assume you failed at homeschooling—you merely covered different work than what the exam addressed. You can make a mental note to be sure to cover that topic in the near future, and return to your normal homeschooling routine.

However, if you see that your children seem truly to be having trouble in a certain area (for instance, your child scores in the lowest 10th percentile on the reading section of the exam, even though she is familiar with the testing format and was feeling terrific on test day), you will need to take a closer look at what is going on. Perhaps you had suspected that she wasn't where she needed to be when it came to reading. This may be the flag you need to seek professional evaluation.

Poor results shouldn't be reason to feel you failed. Instead, they should be merely another tool you, the homeschool teacher, can use to be an even better teacher. As you see from the above examples, you can use the results to adjust your curriculum, to discover a problem you had missed, or to confirm one you had suspected. All teachers use evaluation tools, so don't feel bad when results aren't what you had hoped they would be. Instead, be glad you have a head's up, and follow up with the appropriate action.

However, in the end you may be the kind of person who thinks that tests are overall a poor tool for assessing a child's knowledge. This may well be true—there is no perfect tool. However, if you are forced to administer exams regardless of your feelings, do so, but keep in mind that it is how you use the tool that matters in the end. If you believe the test is less than perfect, that is fine: Do what you must to comply with your state's homeschooling laws and opt to discard the results, if you feel it best, or use what positive you *do* receive. If you are honest with yourself, there is likely some benefit, even if it is paltry in your eyes.

Ultimately, your children have far more knowledge than what their test scores indicate about them, and a number on an exam doesn't define who they are or what they are capable of. The scores are merely a tool to be used to assess where your children are academically and to perhaps catch a problem you may have otherwise not caught at the time.

There are other benefits as well. Perhaps test results can help mark a potential learning disability, something you perhaps suspected but dismissed. Seeing how your children perform in contrast to others may help you recognize the depth of a problem, lest it merely reflect a topic you hadn't covered. Though some parents view the labeling of children with learning disabilities with suspicion, it is a good idea to be alert for any specific problems that interfere with learning. It would be unfortunate for a child to miss out on learning to read when the only impediment is the child's vision or a hearing deficit. When a parent suspects a serious learning problem, testing may be one tool that can help that parent sort out whether there is really a problem.

An experienced first grade teacher can have a child read a little and make a reasonable judgment as to whether the child reads as well as the average first grader or is a little ahead or behind the average. But most parents don't have the experience to know how to do that. Instead, they might choose to have their children take a standardized test, even if it is not required by their state. Some homeschoolers worry that they may one day be required to prove the effectiveness of their homeschooling program to a third party, for instance, if they have an ex-spouse who disapproves of their choice to homeschool their children. They want to have test results available just in case they're ever needed. Test results may also prove helpful if some day the kids attend a traditional school.

Just as there are homeschoolers who appreciate the benefits of standardized tests, there are those who feel that standardized tests do more harm than good and only submit to them if the law compels them to do so. Such parents believe these tests are inadequate at evaluating their children's knowledge and skills or that they interfere with their family's relaxed, natural approach to learning. They doubt the benefit of administering what they feel is a substandard evaluation tool or the value of interrupting a child who is devouring every book on ancient civilizations that he or she can in order to make the child practice for the test.

Some children, particularly in unschooling families, learn things according to timetables that are vastly different from the norm. An unschooled eight-year-old math whiz might master material several grade levels beyond his age-mates, while his reading skills temporarily lag behind theirs by a couple of years. Unschooling purists are reluctant to interfere with their children's passionate study in an area of their choosing in order to study another subject merely for testing purposes, trusting that their children's passion for knowledge will eventually lead to studying all they need to know.

Arranging for Testing

If you've determined that you are going to have your children tested— because it is legally required or because you feel an evaluation would be useful—you need to consider your testing options. There are a number of ways a homeschooling parent can arrange for their children to undergo standardized testing. These options for fulfilling requirements vary from state to state, so learn your state's statutes to ensure you are administering a test that is in compliance with your local mandates.

If you live in a state that gives parents multiple options for complying with testing requirements, decide what you want to accomplish by testing, and choose whatever test situation meets your goals. If you hope to have your children become accustomed to testing in a group setting, you will want to find an option that fulfills this. If you merely want to satisfy the minimum requirement, find the easiest way to accomplish this. If you feel, though, that it is important to see where your children are academically, you may want to have a private test administered, where the exam is administered in a familiar setting or one-on-one so as not to skew the children's results in any way.

First consider who will be administering the exam. Some states specify who may conduct the testing, while others do not. Our state recommends, but doesn't require, that someone other than the parent administer the test. Some may even require that the testing take place in a conventional classroom setting, and in this instance parents can turn to a local public or private school that may allow their children to be tested there. If you aren't required to take this avenue, you could administer the test yourself if this doesn't violate the rules of the test you choose. Or, if you belong to a homeschooling group, you could perhaps hire a professional to administer the exam. There are professional teachers who supplement their income by administering standardized tests to homeschooled students. If for some reason you don't want your children tested in a group situation, consider hiring a teacher to administer the exam privately.

Some parents want their children to gain experience in a group testing situation, reasoning that they might attend public or private school some time in the future or may have to take tests in classrooms when they later attend college. Other parents see testing as one of the aspects of conventional school programs with which they disagree and are confident that their intense involvement in their homeschooled children's learning gives them the ability to evaluate their children's progress without formal testing. These parents, if given the choice, will probably administer the tests themselves in order to keep it as low-key as possible.

Which Test?

Your state's legal requirements may determine which test you must administer, but in many instances this is not the case. Some allow the parent to choose the test, sometimes specifying what subjects it must cover. There are a number of tests that are used by homeschoolers, and for the most part they are quite similar to one another in the skills they test. The California Achievement Test (CAT), the Stanford Achievement Test, the Metropolitan Achievement Test, and the Iowa Test of Basic Skills can all be purchased by parents through the mail or online. You may want to obtain information on several of them so that you can learn the particulars of each one, noting things such as length of testing, rules for administering the test, cost, type of results reporting you can expect, and turnaround time.

You will note that the time allotted for testing can vary quite a bit. For example, in the high school years, the CAT is about two hours longer than the MAT. You will have to decide whether you are more concerned about the depth of skills testing or about the rapidity with which your child can complete the exam. Additionally, some exams require administration by a college graduate. Make sure you meet all the criteria so that your results will be valid. Finally, whichever test you use, they will be more useful to you if you have your kids take the same test each year.

To give you an example of some of the specific differences, the Iowa Basic Skills exam must be administered by someone who holds a bachelor's degree, is a certified teacher, or who has been a full time teacher in a conventional school. The Stanford exam must also be administered by someone holding a bachelor's degree; however, the person must additionally be listed as a pre-approved tester. The Stanford allows an option to administer a complete battery, or just select portions of the test. Again, you must look at the requirements of your state, as well, when making the decision.

What to Do with the Results

Once you receive the test results, you may wonder how to interpret them. Test results can have serious effects on parents who worry if their children perform poorly or who are thrilled when their children perform extremely well.

First, recognize that tests are just one tool that can help evaluate your children's academic achievement and shouldn't be the deciding factor in your children's educational future. If your children scored poorly on a portion of the test simply because they are learning things in a different sequence from the one assumed by the test designers, obviously this poor showing isn't cause for alarm. If you reviewed the test in advance, you probably expected that your children wouldn't score well in some areas due to a lack of exposure to that specific topic of study.

Sometimes an unexpectedly low score frightens parents, causing them to doubt their homeschooling competence or worry that their children have learning disabilities. If this happens, slow down and take a look at the big picture before concluding that you have a serious problem. Suppose, for instance, that your voracious reader of scientific journals and college-level science texts scores poorly on the reading comprehension portion of a test. Look a little further and see if you can find a reasonable explanation for the unexpectedly low score. There are many factors that can cause a child to test poorly. Young children are less likely to understand the implications of testing and often do not grasp the need to focus on performing well. Or perhaps the child had a headache, was excited about his impending birthday party, or found the reading passages to be exceptionally boring because he's used to reading higher-level material on a regular basis. Maybe he had trouble sitting still for the time the testing required or couldn't keep his attention on a seemingly pointless test. He might have daydreamed for a few minutes between answering test questions instead of quickly moving on to the next one, thus affecting how much he could complete. Maybe he spent half of the testing period rereading a story or poem he enjoyed, instead of moving on to the next one right away. Homeschooled kids who are unaccustomed to testing often need a little coaching in basic test-taking skills that most of us take for granted. Perhaps all you need to do is coach him on these skills before your next standardized test time arrives.

In general, achievement testing done in the younger grades is considered to be less reliable than that done in the later grades. If you're unsure as to whether there's a good reason as to why your children scored badly and question if you are perhaps wrong about their skill level, take a closer look at your children's performance in daily tasks. Try discussing with your children books they have read if they scored poorly in reading comprehension. Do they seem to understand what is going on? Additionally, you might make a point of finding out whether they can easily understand and follow written instructions. If not, this could explain what went wrong on the test. However, if your children's performance in the home setting makes it clear to you that the test results don't give an accurate assessment of their achievement, don't worry if that area on the exam fails to reflect this. Chalk it up to their lack of experience with test taking, and make sure they're better prepared next time around.

Preparing Your Children for Testing

A homeschooled child isn't likely to be prepared for the stringent requirements of standardized tests. Nor are homeschooled kids typically familiar with the fill-in-the-blank, match the columns, or color-in-the-little-dots with a #2 pencil approach typical of such exams.

One way to address this without interfering with your current school plan is to occasionally play word games in which your children will fill in a blank. You can do this orally at first, then later write up one or two examples now and then, to prepare your children for encountering this format on an exam. Do the same with circles. You can draw three pictures or words, draw circles underneath them, and have your children identify the right answer to a question you ask by having them fill in the correct circle.

To prepare your children for the reading comprehension sections of the exam, ask many questions when your children read books to help them grow accustomed to answering the types of questions one finds in these sections. This would include questions about major plot directions, what a particular character did, or what the overall point of the story was.

Furthermore, you can order practice tests along with your exams so that your children can get a good idea of what to expect on test day. Or you could opt to purchase one of the products that can aid your children in test preparation. Laura has used Building Thinking Skills, a workbook designed to help children become familiar with multiple-choice questions and eliminating options. She has found that this helped her children feel more comfortable taking exams.

Finally, if you want to be sure you've covered all that will be on the exam, make sure you've consulted standard Scope and Sequence charts, as most exams reflect the correlating course work they typically list.

Some Sources for Standardized Tests

McGuffy Testing Service
P.O. Box 155
Lakemont, GA 30552
706-782-7709

Bayside School Services
P.O. Box 250
Kill Devil Hills, NC 27948
252-441-5351
800-723-3057

They offer the California Achievement Test and also sell guidebooks that tell which skills are covered on each test section for the different grades.

Center for Talented Youth
The Johns Hopkins University
3400 N. Charles St.
Baltimore, MD 21218
(410) 516-8301 / (410) 516-0108 fax
http://www.jhu.edu/gifted/edplan/

This center provides testing and other educational services and focuses primarily on highly intelligent kids who are underachievers. A child can take the STEP (Sequential Tests of Educational Progress) and SCAT (School and College Abilities Test) at one of some 250 testing centers nationwide via computer.

Family Learning Organization
P.O. Box 7247
Spokane, WA 99207-0247
(509) 467-2552

A source for the California Achievement Test and the Metropolitan Achievement Test.

CHAPTER 7

Learning Every Minute

✔ Impulse learning

✔ Units out of the blue

Congratulations! You've moved past all the necessary legal, organizational, and methodological issues and are ready to begin homeschooling. Now you can look at what your days will be like.

Homeschooling can be much more than just burying one's head in a textbook each morning. In fact, textbooks don't have to play a prominent role at all if you prefer not to use them. Our daily lives are teeming with opportunities for learning. If you look at your life closely, you will realize there are a myriad of teachable moments each day. When you check your car's oil, you can discuss why a car needs oil or where oil comes from, for example. Or you can explain why you add baking soda when you bake a cake. The possibilities are endless. You will discover that if you learn to watch for teachable moments when they present themselves, your children will learn all sorts of things and are likely to develop a love of learning along the way.

What they learn will not always coincide with typical scope and sequence, but does that really matter in the long run? When your child reaches adulthood, will it matter whether he learned to tell time at age four or six? Or whether cursive writing wasn't mastered until sixth grade, while algebra was studied in fifth? Sure, your child may miss a few questions on the standardized test if he doesn't learn according to prevailing customs, but this may not be a problem in your situation. You are the principal, and you are aware that you have 12 long years in which to teach your child. It's your decision as to whether or not you will indulge Sally's yearning to learn Web design before she's mastered her multiplication tables.

Impulse Learning

It's no great secret that people learn best when they are studying something they are passionate about. Unschooling families exploit this fact every day. Though your homeschooling plan may call for certain information to be learned at certain times, make sure you leave some room for impulse learning. One of the benefits of homeschooling is that it offers extraordinary flexibility. So it would be a shame to be so schedule bound that you miss out on teachable moments. No matter what your style, whether your homeschool operates with military precision or your approach is more laissez-faire, don't forget that your schedule is just a tool to help you get a job done. Make it work for you as you wish, but don't become a slave to it.

Teachable moments can happen in a variety of settings and circumstances. One evening, while a mother is boiling water for pasta, a five-year-old girl points at the steam issuing from the pot and says "Look, mommy! It's smoke!" The astute homeschooling mom recognizes this as a teachable moment and capitalizes on it.

"It does look a lot like smoke, Amanda, but it's actually steam. That water is so hot that some of it turns into steam. It's kind of like a little cloud over the pasta pot." If time allows, the mother might grab an ice cube out of the freezer and say something like "Ice is water, too. We have three different kinds of water now. We have ice, liquid water, and steam." Amanda might ask a question or two, and by the time the exchange ends, she's got the beginnings of an understanding about states of matter, and it all happened before the linguine was done.

Another example of a teachable moment occurs as a mother sits at her desk writing checks to pay bills. Her nine-year-old, wanting some company, asks, "Whatcha doin' Mom?" She replies that she's paying bills, and returns to her task, but then realizes she almost let a teachable moment pass by. She thinks better of it, and lays down her pen.

"See Chris, this is the electric bill. Right here it shows how much electricity our family used last month. This is the telephone bill, and here's the MasterCard bill." Chris might just shrug his shoulders and go on his way; but on the other hand, he might ask his mother how credit cards work, and the two could end up having an informative discussion about credit, interest, and debt. Perhaps she could show him an example of how interest is calculated on a simple interest loan. Since she had explained debt to him, she realized she might as well explain how credit works, important information many children learn in early adulthood, oftentimes when it's too late. Because Chris initiated this "lesson," he will likely retain this knowledge, not even viewing it as school but as something interesting he learned. Had his mom tried to impart the same information while he was plowing through a series of sci-fi novels, solely because she thought it was time for him to learn this particular piece of knowledge, he might not have taken as great an interest.

Of course, there will inevitably come times when a child expresses an interest in something that you simply don't have the knowledge to discuss intelligently without the aid of reference help nearby, for example, "Mommy, if a great white shark and a Portuguese man-o-war got in a fight, who would win?" Don't worry. No one can be an expert in all fields of knowledge. What can you do? If you don't happen to have a shark or jellyfish expert to consult, you could say, "I don't know, but I'm sure it would be a mess! All those tentacles, yuck! We can look it up on our next library trip, though." Just by listening to the child and sharing in his curiosity, you're conveying the message that learning new things is exciting.

Units Out of the Blue

Random situations can present teachable moments that lead to bigger things. If you find that your children aren't satisfied with the answers you provide, consider allowing the topic to develop into an area that officially joins your curriculum. Some homeschoolers are rather systematic in how they use unit studies, incorporating them into a structured curriculum designed to teach specific topics at set times, according to preset lesson plans. However, others prefer to launch spontaneously into a unit study when the time seems ripe for learning, precisely what some teachable moments can develop into. We like to call these "units out of the blue."

These typically begin with your children's curiosity triggering a conversation. Your answer, instead of closing the subject, captures the children's interest, and the next thing you know, you're on the way to the library to check out books on the topic. Soon enough, you're doing art projects that are related to the topic and researching it on the Internet or seeking out local experts that can add their expertise to the new exploration. Congratulations, you're now involved in a full blown unit—out of the blue!

Units out of the blue are not part of a school plan, so they can make your homeschooling "untidy" because topics are covered in a haphazard fashion. Some parents just can't cope with that sort of unpredictability, but others find it to be a very relaxed, enjoyable way for children to learn. Faithful unschoolers believe that allowing a child's natural curiosity to spark such adventures in learning is at the heart of what homeschooling should be. If you can be comfortable with the spontaneity of this approach, you may find your homeschooling life is greatly enriched by it. Remember, you don't need to fully embrace the unschooling philosophy to incorporate units out of the blue into your school life. Instead, you can just design your curriculum to allow you the flexibility to incorporate one into your program when it comes up.

CHAPTER 8

Social Stuff

Perhaps the most frequent question a homeschooler hears is, "What about socialization?"

Kids, especially teens, feel the need to be around their peers. If you live in a neighborhood with few children, you may have to get a bit creative to make sure your children have opportunities to meet and interact with their peers.

The types of social settings in which your children find themselves can play a role in determining the sorts of friends they make. Neighborhood and school playmates meet randomly according to geographic location and chance seating arrangements in the classroom. While they may have socioeconomic situations that are similar, these may be the only demographics children would share with friends they meet in such a circumstance.

However, when you homeschool you have an opportunity to better control the setting in which your children meet and befriend others.

While you can't always control the types of children your children interact with, especially when it comes to neighborhood friends, there are ways to increase the likelihood that your child meets others who come from families that hold similar values to your own. People with similar interests and values tend to gravitate to certain groups and by joining one, such as a church group or homeschool support group, you will find that your children will likely make friends with those who are good if not great playmates for them. Of course, there are no guarantees that this will be the case. But if you encourage your children to participate in the following, you may be pleasantly surprised with the results.

Support Groups

If you live in an urban area it is quite likely that there is at least one formal homeschool support group near you, if not many. If you live in a rural area, don't panic—you still may find support groups. See our Appendix for a listing of the official support groups or homeschooling organizations in your state. Contact them to learn of the resources in your area.

You may find that your community has different styles of support groups, which may be religious based, goal oriented (for instance, field trips or social events), or simply groups of homeschoolers who get together informally to discuss ideas and to provide reinforcement and encouragement to their members. Regardless of their structure, such groups offer an opportunity for social interaction in a group setting, or *socialization*. Homeschool parents typically find that attending such groups benefits not only their children, but them as well—homeschooling can be a lonely endeavor if you don't reach out to others! Support groups can be a good first step toward meeting others who are going through or have experienced the same things that you have.

When you join a support group, you'll find that your younger children appreciate the opportunity to meet other youngsters their age who live by similar rules or have lifestyles similar to their own. Hanging out with other homeschooled kids may even be a relief for the younger child, if they've encountered negative feedback from neighborhood friends who are attending traditional schools.

You'll find that your teenagers love support groups *if* it includes others their age. Teenagers have a great need to feel as if they belong, and support groups can go a long way toward filling this need. It helps your teens to realize they are not the only homeschooled teens out there.

Support groups often try to get teens working together on educational projects of some sort and may even organize science fairs, field days, and musical or dramatic productions. Sometimes a parent or community member will offer a semiformal class such as art or foreign language, and they may take educational field trips together or even hold high school proms and graduation ceremonies. The types of activities vary, so interview a group you are considering joining to find out exactly what they do to better determine if it will meet the needs of your family.

Even if you can't find a group that seems perfect, you may want to join one nonetheless, as you will find that support groups can offer the camaraderie and reinforcement you need as a homeschooling parent. We encourage you to visit your area support groups to better determine if this option is for you and to learn new homeschooling tips and suggestions.

Church

If your family belongs to a church, you will often find that your church offers a wealth of opportunity for social interaction. Some homeschoolers choose to make church the core of their social life, as they feel confident that the church social circle will bring them into contact with many individuals who share their spiritual and moral beliefs. Most churches have organizations that provide activities for children and teens that give them opportunities to get to know kids their own age in a healthy environment.

If your children's social life centers around church friends, it is likely that their friends will have values similar to those of your family. If your religion is an important aspect of your family life, then your children's participation in these activities will reinforce these values. You may even be fortunate enough to learn that other members of your church family are homeschoolers and, if this is the case, learn whether or not your church has a homeschool support group. If there are several homeschooling families in your church community, and you don't have a homeschool support group, you may want to consider starting one yourself!

Community Organizations

You will quickly discover that there are many community organizations and activities that provide social interaction for your children within a group setting. Even if you don't find a support group you are comfortable with, there are other structured groups you may want to explore. For instance, 4-H clubs are inexpensive groups that will provide a wide range of learning activities for your children, while giving them the opportunity to interact socially. Aimed at boys and girls ages 9 to 19 (though some groups have programs for younger children as well), the groups initially were begun to help teach techniques of agriculture and home economics, as well as to promote high ideals regarding such topics as leadership and civics. They were begun by the Cooperative Extension Service of the U.S. Dept of Agriculture on land granted by colleges and universities. These groups are run by volunteers under the guidance of the Cooperative Extension Service.

The program has now spawned similar groups in over 85 countries and has extended its scope to include cross-cultural education and exchange. Call your local Cooperative Extension Service to learn if there is a group near you. With over 5.5 million members in the United States, you are likely to find one.

4-H clubs are only one type of community group you may want to explore. There are also boy and girl scouting groups, YWCAs and YMCAs, and community center programs. To get a better idea of what kinds of programs are available in your area, contact your local Y.

CHAPTER 9

Tools of the Trade

There are tools for almost every trade, and this is true of homeschooling as well. Some are more obvious, for instance, the need for a teacher and students, as well as pens, pencils, notebooks—all the basic staples that come to mind. Additionally, one might think of desks, though many homeschoolers find a dining room table can work just as well or even prefer to hold lessons in their backyard or while sitting in a circle on their living room floor. Remember, flexibility is one of the advantages of homeschooling.

Once you have the basic tools, you can homeschool. However, there are some tools that, while not essential, can certainly add to your homeschooling experience. There are certain ones we can't imagine being without since they so greatly enhance our homeschooling experience, and therefore we want to share them with you.

Reference Books

Perhaps the most obvious tool is the reference library that has a good dictionary and thesaurus as its core and that is also rounded out by a good set of encyclopedias. If you have a computer, you will find that encyclopedias on CD-Rom are a fraction of the cost of a full set. You can, on the other hand, find older encyclopedia sets for almost no cost at all at local used bookstores or yard sales. Either of these options can help you create a dynamite reference library for your homeschool at a relatively low cost.

While you may think these things unnecessary if you visit your library often, we find that having these resources at our fingertips allows our kids to find answers to their questions when they want them. Waiting until the next library trip may mean they forget about the topic entirely. It also empowers *you*—now you can tell your older children "Great question, why not go look it up and see what else you can learn about it?" Laura's son Brandon has heard this phrase so often that he now just goes to the encyclopedia on his own, without prompting, one of the goals many parents dream of achieving when they homeschool!

Field Guides

If the idea of a home reference library appeals to you, you might want to add some field guides to round out your collection. Peterson's field guides to birds, plants, and trees are great for your young nature lovers. Or supplement your library with reference guides for astronomy or weather—whatever intrigues your family. Remember, books don't have to cost a fortune. Check out your local used bookstores and library sales. You'll likely find some great bargains.

Maps and Globes

Maps and globes add an important component to your homeschooling classroom. How better to teach your children about the world than to show them exactly where a Bengal tiger comes from? Or where their favorite rock band is touring? You can find inexpensive maps and globes in discount stores, and you can oftentimes get great maps out of *National Geographic Magazine*.

Microscopes

Microscopes are another great addition to your homeschool, if you can afford them. This tool can help your children gain an understanding of the microscopic world and an appreciation for how much is going on right under their noses. Many science companies sell used ones, and you may also try your local school system to see if they have any used ones for sale. If all else fails, see if your local community college will allow for the occasional visit to the lab. This is not unheard of, and would be a field trip that many children would just love!

Arts and Crafts Box

Many homeschoolers find that arts and crafts projects are enjoyable and that incorporating creative projects into their day can add a nice dimension to their studies. A big box of scraps of fabric, construction paper, Styrofoam, scissors, markers, crayons, and glue can be all the encouragement your children need to bring out the Picasso or Monet in them. Furthermore, these can be used to reinforce subjects you are studying. Say Sally just loves reading about rainbows. You could perhaps show her how a prism can be used to create a rainbow, and then have her create her own with either crayons, markers, paints, or even fabrics in the craft box. Having all the necessary items in one place makes this a cinch.

Outside Resources

Tools don't necessarily have to be things you own, but can be things you use as well. Homeschoolers may turn to a variety of places to supplement their child's education. If you take the time to dig a little, you'll discover a wealth of community resources. Obviously the type of resources available to you will depend upon where you live, but most homeschoolers have access to a public library, which often has fun activities for children. For many of us, there are so many community activities that we have to be careful to avoid overscheduling our kids. When we consider a community activity, we try to be realistic about its value. It may not be worth the 30-minute drive to story hour at the library unless there's something really special about that story hour. However, driving 30 minutes for your children to attend a children's book discussion club may be a great use of time if it gets your shy child interacting with other kids or kindles the interest of a reluctant reader. So, look at what your community offers, and then choose wisely.

Community Colleges

Many local community colleges allow older teens to take courses there. If you are unfamiliar with a particular subject your teen wants to study and don't feel up to the challenge of taking a crash course in an area such as physics or calculus, such classes can be a viable option. Admission policies such as age and prerequisites vary, but you can learn these details by contacting the admissions office of any college your teen is considering. In our state, 16-year-old students may take community college courses, but students in a degree program would get first pick of classes, so availability of slots for high school students is limited. While there may be some restrictions, it is worth taking the time to learn about this option. Sometimes teens worry about how they will fare in a classroom setting, but often taking a course or two reassures them that they can do just fine.

People

Don't overlook the knowledge and skills within your own community and extended family. Cultivate the habit of looking out for human educational resources whenever you make a new acquaintance. Oftentimes, friends and family members can be the basis for what become fascinating field trips.

For instance, one weekend one of Julie's patients revealed that he owned a fish hatchery business. In the course of conversation she mentioned that she had children, and he enthusiastically invited her to bring them to see his hatchery operation. This is one of many times that we experienced this sort of unexpected opportunity, so keep yourself open to such opportunities as they present themselves.

Real stories or hands-on experience impart a much deeper understanding of history or of how things work than a child would gain from simply reading textbooks, and they make it more exciting as well.

Museums, Zoos, and Planetariums

If you live in an urban area, you are likely to have resources such as museums, zoos, and planetariums nearby. There are many different ways the homeschooling family can use these resources. The most basic involves taking your children there and letting them explore to their heart's content.

Young children, in particular, often enjoy viewing the same exhibits or shows many times. Parents can lend a hand by helping the children read the related information posted at the exhibit and answering their questions. If you encourage your children to enjoy the process of discovery, you may find the pleasure is contagious.

Try making up little games when visiting a natural science museum with young children. For instance, you can go "mammal spotting" in a science museum or zoo. Simply explain what a mammal is, and play it like "I spy." Julie had a terrific time playing this with Isabel recently. Whenever they approached a furry four-legged animal, she got to cry out "mammal alert!" To add to the fun, Julie would occasionally admire a hawk or an eel, exclaiming, "Oh, what an interesting mammal," enjoying her child's delight in Mom's being so silly.

While you are mammal spotting with your younger kids, encourage your older ones to learn deeper details about an exhibit, perhaps with the plan of compiling a report based on the information.

Sometimes museums, zoos, or planetariums offer science classes with strong kid appeal and hands-on activities of all kinds. Our natural history museum offers regular "Meet the Animals" programs during which a museum staff member introduces a variety of creatures, providing all sorts of interesting facts about them. They also present several science programs each week on topics such as weather, the water cycle, or the wetlands. Such programs allow children to have an interactive science experience, as well as to experience using gadgets they wouldn't have otherwise had an opportunity to see, such as a Van der Graft generator that teaches about static electricity, or a cloud-making device.

Art museums, zoos, and planetariums are all exciting, and each offers an equally wide variety of opportunities. If you have these resources nearby, you may well benefit from incorporating them into your home-school program.

Computers in the Homeschool

While owning a computer is not essential to homeschooling, having one can sure make life simpler and more interesting. It is the one item we believe a homeschooler should make an effort to purchase if it is at all within their means. While we are firm believers in finding inexpensive substitutes for materials whenever possible (such as using M&Ms instead of expensive math manipulatives), there is just no substitute for the computer. As prices on technology continue to fall, computers will become a more viable option for families. If it's impossible for you to purchase one, try to find one for your children to use, perhaps at your local library, a community center, or at a neighbor's house.

Why is the computer such a valuable resource for homeschoolers? Computers can be used to reinforce basic skills, coax reluctant learners, relieve burnout, and provide a welcome change of pace from the daily grind, all while your children are learning to use a piece of hardware they are likely to need to be familiar with by the time they enter the workforce. This chapter will explain how to incorporate computer use into your homeschooling life.

Educational CD-Roms

Perhaps the most obvious use of the computer in the homeschool is for incorporating fun educational software into your school routine. There are some terrific educational CD-Roms on the market, and they can help reinforce just about any subject imaginable. Companies such as The Learning Company and Davidson put out stellar programs for younger children that will leave your child feeling as if he's been playing, not learning. Let your kids enjoy the games, and smile to yourself with the secret knowledge that they are getting educational value from their playtime.

For older children, there are CD-Roms that can help them learn advanced subjects such as chemistry, anatomy and physiology, and calculus—subjects that typically intimidate some homeschool parents. The interactive elements found in many of these games also serve to make the subject fun and exciting, something that can be difficult to do when merely using textbooks.

We have found the following to work for us.

- **Try foreign language software for your computer.** There are some terrific programs that even work on your pronunciation. They typically have great interactive games with excellent graphics. Encourage your child to use the software regularly, as it helps reinforce vocabulary retention.

- **Math games for drill practice.** Laura allows her boys educational "free time" from 1 to 3 p.m. during which they can opt to spend extra time using educational software. They frequently choose math games such as Treasure Math Storm, or Math Blaster, and she has found they retain basic math skills almost effortlessly.

- **Encourage your kids to enjoy educational software in their free time.** Laura's boys love the School House Rock CD-Roms and play them frequently. They've learned everything from how a bill becomes a law to what a conjunction is through these exciting CD-Roms. Magic School Bus software is also very popular in their home, and Laura feels it does a wonderful job introducing her boys to some basic science concepts—and the games are a lot of fun, too. She doesn't have to encourage the boys to play, as they are clamoring to do so on their own.

Using E-Mail and Internet Messaging for Writing Practice

Using E-Mail

The ability to use educational software is only one of the many advantages of using a computer in your homeschool. You can also, for instance, use your computer to encourage your child to practice his writing skills.

Children love getting mail, so corresponding via e-mail or Internet messaging can be a fun way for your children to practice writing while ensuring that they have a box full of mail. Remind your children that the more letters they write, the more responses they will get! If your children have trouble figuring out what to write, tell them to just write about their day and ask others about how their day went. However, you will want to scan some of the letters before they hit the send button so that you can help them edit for spelling and grammatical errors. As they get used to writing, encourage them to use different adjectives and verbs to make their letters more colorful.

Using Internet Messaging

E-mail is a terrific way to teach your children to write. However, many children also enjoy using real-time chat software, such as AOL's Instant Messaging, ICQ, or Yahoo's Yahoo! chat. We like using AOL's IM because of the ability to exert parental control—for instance, by choosing the option to block all but those you allow on your list. While the Internet can be a terrific tool, you must make sure your children explore this medium in a way that is safe, especially when they are communicating with others.

Once you know who your children are communicating with, and set some ground rules about interacting with strangers, your children will be free to begin using Internet Messaging. One benefit of real-time chatting is your children grow inspired to spell better and faster to keep pace with the conversation. They'll also begin to learn the general location of the keys on the keyboard, a great segue into learning to type. You may want to purchase typing software, as well, to further encourage them to learn to type.

Getting the Most Out of Your Word Processing Program

Another way to use your computer to encourage your children to master their writing skills is to have them use your word processing program to write stories or keep a journal. With younger children you can use a program such as Davidson's Kid Works word processing software, with which they can even illustrate their writing and print it out in book form.

Don't be afraid to let them use spell-check, so that they learn how to correct their mistakes. Tell them to jot down the words they misspelled in a notebook that you keep next to the computer, and you can use that to generate this week's spelling list, if you'd like. Let them use grammar check, too, so they can see where they went wrong grammatically; but make sure you sit with them while they do it so that you can explain the "why" behind the corrections.

Once your children have written a story, they can then print it and bind it in a nice folder, or create a cover with construction paper or cardboard. Once they have mastered the basics of word processing and page design, you may want to encourage them to try a program such as Illustrator or Publisher. With these programs they can learn to lay out their work professionally, allowing them to create elaborate newsletters, books, and projects of all sorts. They can even make things like business cards, letterhead, and flyers. If they have an entrepreneurial streak they could even start their own small neighborhood printing business. The possibilities are almost endless with programs such as these. Not only will they be proud of all the different things they can do, but they will have learned a marketable skill as well—and gotten writing practice to boot!

Internet Research

The Internet allows you to search across the world for information on a particular topic without leaving your desk. While an encyclopedia can give you tons of information, the Internet can provide you with more updated information, a variety of perspectives, and a wide sampling of information.

Your children can start by visiting the most commonly used search engines, such as:

- www.yahooligans.com (especially for kids!)
- www.yahoo.com
- www.Snap.com
- www.northernlight.com
- www.hotbot.com
- www.askjeeves.com
- www.google.com

Once you find a helpful website, you may want to check out the websites they link to, since they may be equally informative as the one you are currently viewing, though this isn't always the case.

If your search is too broad (e.g., "Astronomy"), you may need to narrow it, since the number of sites out there on any topic could number in the millions. In this instance, you would want to perhaps put the narrowest piece of information into the search request box (such as "the Milky Way"). If you go to askjeeves.com, you can enter the search request in the form of a question, such as "Where is the Milky Way located?" which some people find useful. The Internet has a vast amount of information, much of which can be very helpful. There is one caveat, though. Know the source of the material you are looking at. For instance, anyone at all can create a Web page. If you want real information on, say, how to prevent heart disease, you are likely to find more reliable data at a website hosted by the Mayo Clinic or the American Heart Association as opposed to John Doe's Heart Healthy page. It may be that John Doe is an expert on the prevention of heart disease—then again, he could be a paranoid schizophrenic who gives advice that is less than credible, if not completely wrong.

Web Publishing

Once your children have explored the Net and garnered a better idea of what it is about, they may want to become part of the World Wide

Web themselves by creating their own Web page. Wouldn't it be great for them to see their work published? Well, your children can experience the exhilaration of being published on the Internet. Their site can be a platform where they express their thoughts on a myriad of issues. They can publish poetry, short stories, information about their favorite literary or television character, or start a fan club, right there on the Internet. They can use their site to help others, too. Perhaps they could create a forum for other homeschooled kids or a site for people who want to learn about the spotted owl. Whatever they want to do, they can—that is the beauty of the Internet (and the danger, too!).

Web publishing isn't very hard. Most Internet service providers (ISP) offer free Web space if you use their service. Then you use an HTML editor to create your website. The HTML editors make it so easy that even a very young child can create a website. So, encourage your children to express themselves!

If your ISP doesn't offer free Web space, check out one of the following sites:

- www.geocities.com
- www.angelfire.lycos.com
- www.tripod.lycos.com

These sites will walk you through setting up a website and offer you places to obtain all kinds of graphics and animations, and so on. To learn more about creating a website using HTML, the language with which one writes Web pages, your child can visit the award-winning site www.lissaexplains.com, which many children have used to learn Web page design successfully. This is an interesting and kid-friendly website that you may find helpful, too.

As you can see, there are many ways in which a computer can enhance your homeschooling life. We've only listed a few of the many possibilities; the opportunities are endless. If you are unsure about the role a computer can play in your life, try using one in your library or at an "Internet cafe" to see if this is something you may find helpful.

At Home with Language Arts

The ability to read and write well is the cornerstone of a good education. A strong reader has the tools for learning nearly anything she wants to know, and a skillful writer can communicate effectively using written language. If you help your children develop solid language skills, you will provide them with a strong foundation for their future learning.

This chapter demonstrates some playful ways to approach reading and writing with your children so that they will learn painlessly and naturally.

Teach Your Children to Read

If you instill in your children a love of reading, you will have given them a key to learning. Filling your home with books, reading to your children frequently, and letting them see that you enjoy reading will help ensure that they become good readers.

Be sure to show your reading children how much freedom this ability gives them. Point out that they can now read directions to their new game all by themselves. They can look in the newspaper to see what time their favorite TV show is on. Children love this independence. A benefit to the parents is that a child who can read independently can be reading social studies and science while you are busy teaching your younger children.

Reading can be an adventure for your children. You will discover that not only do you enjoy this special time together, but that home-schooling becomes easier once your children learn to read.

The Great Debate

For decades educators have debated the relative merits of phonics versus the whole language approach to teaching reading. The phonics approach teaches the child to "crack the code" of written language by using the sounds that letters and groups of letters represent. The whole language approach immerses the child in language, teaching him sight words, and incorporating a variety of reading-related activities.

Teach Reading with Phonics

Advocates of phonics think children need to acquire the "word attack" skills that phonics instruction provides. Without phonics, they believe, a child will not have the skills to decode the more challenging words that are introduced in the later elementary years.

There are many ways to teach phonics to your children, and you can do it in just a few minutes each day. You may decide you want to purchase a formal phonics program, but it really isn't necessary. There are many books available that can be used to teach the basic phonics sounds.

Whether you decide to use a phonics program or not, you may find some of the following helpful:

- **Exaggerate the sounds at the beginning of words.** When you hand them a cookie, say, "Would you like a c-c-c-ookie?" Then say, "Cookie starts with 'c,' " saying the sound rather than the letter name. Ask if they can think of other words that start with "c." After they master the letter sounds, progress to sound blends like "ch" or "sh."

- **Rhymes are great for teaching your children phonics.** You can ask them what words sound like "cake" and lead them to discover rhymes, such as "bake," "lake," and "take." Make this a game, and see who runs out of rhyming words first.

- **Play "Sound of the Day" with your children.** At the breakfast table, introduce a new sound. Choose a word, like "boy." Ask if they know what sound "boy" starts with. If they don't, tell them it is "b." Throughout the day, you'll be giggling as you look for other words that start with the "Sound of the Day." Keep track of who comes up with the most. Make it fun, finding silly words that start with the sound of the day.

- **Once your children have a firm understanding of the letter sounds, and sound blends, show them how to blend them together to make a word.** Explain that knowing these letter sounds is like knowing a secret code. This will make the process more exciting.

- **Go "Sound Hunting."** After you've introduced a few of the letter sounds, toss the cards you taught them with on the table and ask them to get one for you—that is, "Get me a 'b,' " or "get me an 's.' " Whenever they get the correct sound, praise them. You may opt to reward them with a sticker when they get them all right.

- **Play "Climbing the Stairs."** Stand at the bottom of a staircase. Using flashcards (or the sounds written on paper), show your children a sound. If your children correctly identify the sound, they can go up one step. When they get to the top, they get a "prize," such as a gold star, sticker, or a special privilege.

Using the Whole Language Approach

Whole language approaches involve immersing children in print. That is, providing them with a variety of reading material and having them read and write a good deal, even in the early stages of reading development.

Most of the everyday language we use is comprised of 500 basic words. Of those 500 words, only 100 of them are used frequently. Teach your children those 100 words, and you will have given them a jump start into reading. We have used these techniques and games to teach sight words, and they have proven to be fun and effective. Try the following:

- **Label items around your house.** Putting labels on pieces of furniture, doors, and appliances will teach your children the words and their meanings. They will see "door" on the door, and learn to associate the word with the object. To make it sillier, try labeling each other's body parts. Seeing mom with a label on her nose will get them laughing!

- **Help your children make a word box.** Give your children a box and tell them this is their *special* box, and it is going to hold a special treasure. It is for their own personal words, words that they have mastered. Have them decorate the box as fancifully as they like, making it their unique hiding place. Each day give them each a word written on a slip of paper. Have them practice saying it. Have them try to use it 20 times in the day. Then, before bedtime, have them deposit it in their box. It then becomes part of their "word treasure." Every day have them review their treasure, and soon the words will truly become theirs!

- **Fish for words.** Fishing for words is a great little game. Write a few of the most common sight words on pieces of paper and attach them to paper clips. Then make a fishing rod and line out of a small stick, string, and magnet. Use the fishing rod to "fish" for words. Every time a fish gets "caught," the child has to read the word (with your help if needed).

- **Play "Sight Word Bingo."** Make bingo cards using the 100 most common words. Then write the 100 words on slips of paper and place them in a bowl. Pull one from the bowl, and read it out loud. Your children can use pennies, raisins, or M&Ms to mark their cards if they have the word you've called. They win when they have marked a whole row.

- **Play "Word Hunt."** Hide little pieces of paper with sight words on them. If working with an older child, feel free to list up to five words per slip. Each time your child finds a hidden slip, have him read the word(s), with your help, if necessary. The excitement of searching for the slips makes this game fun for a young child.

Teaching Writing in the Elementary School Years

Even before your children have mastered reading, you can begin teaching them to write. Help them create their own journal by decorating a notebook, and encourage them to write down a sentence or two each day. They can spell the words phonetically at first, if necessary, and you can use this opportunity to show them the correct spellings.

You can give your children practice "writing" before they can read or write by having them "write" stories orally. Encourage them to tell stories. If they are at first reluctant, start a story for them, and ask them what they think might happen next. This works well during car trips.

Telling stories gets your children used to organizing their thoughts and helps them understand that a story has a beginning, middle, and end. Later, you can teach your children how to get these thoughts down on paper.

There are many other ways to encourage your children to write, and they are far more enjoyable than "WHAT I DID ON MY SUMMER VACATION" essays you may remember from your own childhood. Here are some suggestions.

- **Journal writing can be fun.** Have a young child write at least a few sentences each day, and review them with her. Let her know how great she's doing, and gently point out a couple of things she can do next time to make her writing even better.

- **Help your children create their own book.** Children love the idea of seeing their work "published." You can do this on a computer and let them illustrate it with a paint program, or do it in a notebook or a book made of construction paper, using ribbon to hold the pages together. Make sure you let them proudly show grandma and grandpa or a close friend their "published" work.

- **Letter writing can provide lots of writing practice.** Children love to get mail. Encourage your children to write letters to relatives, distant friends, or pen pals. Remind them that the more they send, the more they are likely to receive. E-mail is a wonderful option, too, if you have a computer in your home. Don't overlook the benefits of Internet messaging either. Many children are inspired to spell faster and better to keep pace with online conversations.

- **Show them how they can share information with others.** Encourage your children to write about things that interest them. They can even publish it in a website or send it to magazines which publish children's work.

Teaching Grammar

Good writing requires a clear understanding of the rules of grammar. You can teach your children grammar with the aid of a curriculum such as DailyGrams or Simply Grammar. We mention these curricula because they teach grammar in small doses. They won't overwhelm your children with grammar lessons, but will give them a firm understanding of the rules. You can follow up by correcting their written work when appropriate.

You may prefer, however, to teach grammar as the need arises while your children are writing. When your children are frequently exposed to good writing, they will cull from it much information about how language is used.

Some of the following techniques are good for helping your children master the basic rules of grammar:

- **Have your children play "Editor."** Explain to them that you are going to pretend that they are editors, and you are going to turn in an article for them to edit. When you write the short article, make sure you include enough errors for it to be challenging, but not so many as to overwhelm them.

- **Play "Acting Out Verbs."** Throw a ball at your children and tell them you just 'tossed' them a verb. Then explain that a verb is an action word, and ask them to use the ball to show other examples of verbs. They can, for example, "roll" the ball, "spin" the ball, and "kick" the ball. Try this with play-clay, too. You can "squish" the dough, "roll" the dough, and "break" the dough. Get creative!

- **Play "Find 100 Ways."** This is a game that teaches your children all about adjectives. Begin by describing to them that adjectives are words we use to describe things. Pick an object out and then have them find as many words to describe it as they possibly can. The winner is the person who comes up with the last adjective.

- **Play "Parts of Speech Scavenger Hunt."** This is a fun game which has several variations. You can tell a younger child that he has one minute to look around the room and quickly write down all the nouns he sees. Give him a goal to shoot for: 10, 15, or 20 nouns, for example. You can give an older child a copy of an article or a passage from a book and ask him to circle all the pronouns (or any part of speech you are teaching) on the page.

Your Teen Reader

Your teen will have definite ideas of what he wants to read, but you will want to make sure he reads the sorts of literature required by his educational program. You may want to sit down with him and come up with a plan for the year's reading, with a list of books to be read and target dates for completion.

Your teen's reading list can be composed of textbooks, classic literature, special topic reading related to his studies, and "just plain fun" reading. Don't underestimate the benefit of what appears to be purely recreational reading. Even comic books can help build vocabulary and stimulate the imagination.

You may find some of the following suggestions helpful in encouraging your teen reader:

- Create a reading list together each school year.
- Set a minimum requirement for reading each day.
- Require that he read a certain number of works related to his studies.
- Subscribe to magazines that interest him.
- Create a family book club. Members of the family can read a work and discuss it at a designated time.

• Your goal is to keep your child reading. Encourage your teen to talk with you about what he's read. Don't do this as a drill, but as a natural part of daily conversation. You can easily ask, "Hey, Johnny, that book you're reading looks very interesting. Do you like it so far? What's it about?" Taking an interest in what he's reading may encourage him to read even more.

Your Teen Writer

When it comes to writing, practice makes perfect. The more your teen writes, the better writer she will become. Make writing an important part of her life. If you encouraged her to do journal writing when she was younger, make sure she continues to do so now, though you will not be reading and making corrections in this one. Trust us! There are

Interactive Reading

To encourage your children to begin reading, turn story time into learning time. When you are reading a bedtime story, pick a recurring word (it can be a word as common as "the" or "and") and point it out to your children. Have them read it along with you every time you encounter it.

You can choose a "pattern book," where the first or last sentence is the same on every page. Have your children read that sentence with you, even if they are just chanting it from memory. Make sure to run your finger under each word as they speak it. This will help them make the connection between the symbols on the page and the words you are speaking.

You will also want to ask them questions when you finish reading the story. Don't quiz them, but ask them conversationally. You can ask what they thought of the book, who their favorite characters were, and even if they thought there should've been a different ending. Use this as a springboard into other conversations. You can have them orally rewrite the story or use the same characters to create a new one. The possibilities are endless! Don't forget, though, that the most important part of reading is that you all enjoy it!

many other ways your teen can get practice writing. Try some of the following:

- Have your child complete a piece of writing each day. This way she will grow accustomed to explaining something fully, with a beginning, middle, and end.

- Encourage her to keep records about topics that interest her. Then have her put this information together into a research report.

- If you have a computer, and Internet access, let her create her own website.

- Encourage her to write a letter to the editor of your local newspaper so she may express her opinion in print.

- Encourage her to write an article to submit to a magazine that publishes the work of teens.

- Whatever type of writing your child enjoys, encourage it! The more she writes, the better her skills will be. Tactfully correct her work as you read it, while giving her plenty of encouragement.

At Home with Math

Many homeschooling parents are intimidated by math. Can you teach it successfully? What if you have doubts about your own skills? This isn't an insurmountable problem. With the help of a good math curriculum, you can help your children master math, even if at times you find yourself learning alongside them. Just try not to transfer your own fear of math to your children. Instead, try teaching them to approach it in a fun, playful manner, as a mystery to be solved, a puzzle to answer. If you don't let your kids know that you find math difficult, they may never find it difficult.

With younger children, you can use games for teaching mathematical concepts. For older kids, there are fine math curricula out there that allow children to master the material with only occasional parental assistance. This chapter gives you tips to teach your children math in a nonthreatening way. Give your children a healthy attitude toward math, and you will have given them a precious gift that will serve them well in adult life.

Teaching Math in the Elementary School Years

In the elementary school years there are many ways to make mathematics fun and interesting. With a little imagination, you can create games to teach just about any concept. You can also sneak bits of math learning into your children's day by asking well-placed questions now and then: "John, if you each get half of the jelly beans, how many will each of you have?" or "Susie, I want to double this cookie recipe, so how many cups of flour will I need?"

Manipulatives

Mathematics involves not only counting items, adding, subtracting, multiplying, or dividing them, but also teaching symbols. Your children need to learn, for instance, that the numeral 2 stands for 2 items, such as 2 bananas, 2 cookies, or 2 hands, and can also be expressed by the word "two." How can you help your young children understand these symbols? Begin by using objects, or "manipulatives," to demonstrate this to your children in a concrete way. Give them 5 cookies, and teach them the numeral (and word!) 5. Once they have learned to count using manipulatives, they can begin learning how to add or take away objects from their original group of objects. In other words, if you give Joe 5 cookies, and he eats 2 (subtracts 2), he has 3 cookies remaining. From there, try adding, for instance, "Joe, here is 1 cookie, would you like another? Ok, 1 cookie plus 1 cookie equals 2 cookies." In this simple dialogue you are teaching your child symbols for math as well as how to add or subtract. You'll note that this doesn't necessarily have to be done during a formal math period, but rather could take place over lunch or snack time. You will find that there are many different objects you can use, such as beans, pennies, and Cheerios. You can also buy colorful premade manipulatives based on cube units known as Cuisenaire Rods, which can be purchased alone or along with several workbooks that guide children through using the rods to understand the mathematics basics such as addition, subtraction, and multiplication. Whatever object you use, the idea is to demonstrate visually to your children what you are doing, for example, adding or subtracting cookies, and to show them that we use the symbol (the number itself, and the words "add" or "subtract" to represent this). To demonstrate multiplication, give her 2 cookies 3 times, and divide 6 cookies into 3 piles of 2 to demonstrate division. This helps many children really grasp what it is you are trying to explain to them.

Math Drill

There are some subjects that are best learned by drill, such as multiplication tables, and while it may be hard to think of math drill as fun, there are ways you can make it more challenging and exciting. For instance, you can make a game out of it based upon childhood games such as "Giant Step" or "Mother May I?" Have your children stand in a starting position and ask them questions like, "What is 5×5?" If they answer correctly, they can take a giant step forward. If they do not, they can either stay in the same position or take a step backwards. Or, you can tell them what kind of step they can take if they answer correctly. Perhaps they can hop, or jump, or skip. Make it fun, and give them a goal. Once they reach the finish line, for example, perhaps they can consider math done for the day, or you might reward them with a big hug, break time, or an earned privilege. If you like using star charts or stickers, these can also work well. This is just one of many ways to do math drill. You can try chanting the facts as you are driving in the car, seeing who can say them faster. Or you can call out a problem every time you "spy" something, like a Volkswagen or Honda, for instance, in a variation of the game "I Spy."

Home Shopping Club

A good game for teaching your young child to add is to create a home "store." Take empty boxes of familiar products, such as cereal and oatmeal boxes, empty, cleaned milk or yogurt containers, and so forth, and label them with a "price." Then allow your child to "shop" and let her come to the register. Once there, allow her to do self check-out, adding up how much the items cost. Or you can add them up, have her pay with play money, and show her how the change adds up to be the difference between what she owed and what she handed you to pay for the groceries.

Another variation on this game is to give your children a "shopping list" for your home store and a budget. Their goal is to figure out how much they can spend and to stay within budget. With older children, you can play a more realistic game. Give your children the shopping sales circular from your local market and a budget to stay within. Then have them plan meals—first for one evening only. If they are successful, have them try to plan for a longer period of time, perhaps for a week or even a month. They will be responsible for determining how much they can afford to spend and how to best shop. You may even want to allow them to follow through and shop with you for the food and assist you in cooking it.

Chocolate Chip Math

In Laura's home, Chocolate Chip Math has proven to be a fun and delicious way to teach all the basics—addition, subtraction, multiplication, and division. However, they have taken it one step further by adding a die to the game. Each player rolls the die and then takes the corresponding number of chips. If he has 9 chips and rolls a 6, for example, he takes 6 chips from the center of "chip mountain." He now would have 15 chips but for one complication: No player is allowed to possess more than 10 chips at a time. So, the player must find a way to subtract or give away 5 chips. He can do this by eating them, passing them to another player (who then must rid himself of them on his next turn), or by thinking of a clever way to get rid of them—here, we allowed the kids to let their imaginations run wild—soon they were creating doubles—dividing their 12 chips into 2 piles of 6—and we let them get away with it, thinking they were learning a new concept on their own!

If you're uncomfortable with the idea of letting your child eat chocolate to excess, you can establish a maximum number of chips a player can consume, or even omit them altogether and play with something other than food, such as pennies, pebbles, or beans.

Fraction Games

As demonstrated above, food can be a great manipulative and can be employed to introduce fractions as well. You can use pizza, cakes, or even lasagnas to teach your children how to divide things into halves, quarters, eighths, and so forth. Graham crackers seem to have been designed with this very thought in mind. You can also create your own fraction board games using a heavy piece of cardboard or poster board. Just color a picture of a cake, pie, or pizza, and then make several photocopies, preferably in color. Cut one copy in half, another into quarters, another into eighths, another into tenths, and so forth. Then take turns rolling a die and whatever number the player rolls is how many pieces she can add to the cake until she has a complete one. When the pieces are all used, whoever has completed the most cakes or pizzas wins.

You can also use money to teach fractions. Explain to your children that a dollar is made up of 4 quarters, 10 tenths (dimes), 20 fifths (nickels), and 2 halves (50 cent pieces), or 100 ones (pennies). This helps your children develop an understanding of the concept of division, and reinforces their understanding of money.

Kitchen Cooking Math

When your children are working in the kitchen with you, take this opportunity to introduce or reinforce mathematics concepts. You can do this by simply doubling or halving recipes or by determining what kind of substitutions can be made. Additionally, you can add and subtract: For example, "Jimmy, how many extra servings do we need to make when your soccer team comes over for the cookout?" or "You've added ½ of the flour. How much is left to add?" Don't forget to use kitchen cleaning as a learning opportunity, too. When you dilute something, for instance, by mixing one part bleach with three parts water, and then explain the process to your children, you are teaching mathematical concepts.

Math for Teens

Even parents who sail smoothly through their kids' elementary school years become apprehensive when it's time to school their children in more advanced math topics, such as algebra. If you don't feel very confident in your ability to work the math problems you will be expecting your teen to do, you are likely wondering about how you can teach these very concepts.

The good news is you don't necessarily have to have mastered these topics yourself in order for your teen to become proficient at them. There are other ways of handling these topics, and you will likely want to explore some of them. For instance, you can use one of the usual texts for the subjects and find ways to help the teen learn concepts that he can't quite grasp from reading explanations and examples in the textbook. There are many websites that have free math lessons and practice problems to assist both you and your child, and there's also software available that can help demystify even the more complicated mathematical concepts.

You may even want your teen to use more than one textbook for a subject, so that your child can turn to two different sources to explain the same concept. Sometimes a minor difference in the author's approach to teaching the topic can make a vast difference in your child's ability to grasp it, and having more than one textbook on hand makes this all the more possible. If this seems too costly, watch for high school math books being sold inexpensively at yard sales or used bookstores, or in the attics of friends and relatives. The teen could work his way through one textbook systematically and use the others as references when he encounters a concept that is difficult to grasp.

Another interesting option is the video math courses such as the Chalk Dust math programs. You can also find online courses. If this seems too independent for your teen, and you believe he would benefit from one-on-one teaching, but you don't feel you can handle it, you might recruit a qualified relative to work with him or look into hiring a tutor.

We have found that some homeschooling support groups have a parent member who is willing to conduct a regular math class for a small group of teens. There are many possible ways that you can help your teen learn advanced math topics. So consider your options and try whatever seems to be practical for your family. If your teen starts out working independently with a textbook, but becomes frustrated and hates every minute of it, you can look for a better approach. Keep in mind, you are not stuck using any resource just because you thought it would work. One of the beauties of homeschooling is that you have the freedom to try different approaches and resources until something works.

Here are a few of our favorite math resources for teens. You may want to explore some of these before choosing your approach.

Chalk Dust Math Programs

Each course consists of a series of videotaped math presentations by a math teacher, Dana Mosely. His instructional style is very clear, interesting, and dynamic, and the videos are professionally produced. Each course includes a math text and solutions guide. If necessary, the student can communicate with the teacher via phone or e-mail to get questions answered. It is one of the more expensive ways for a homeschooled teen to learn math, but it is a truly outstanding program.

Saxon Math

This is probably the most popular math program among homeschoolers. It uses a very logical incremental approach and in most cases is essentially self-teaching.

Key to Series (Algebra and Geometry)

Each subject is covered in a set of clear, logically progressing workbooks. They are more suitable for students who are not college bound and do not need college preparatory courses.

Easy Way Series

Each of these inexpensive paperbacks, *Geometry The Easy Way*, or *Calculus The Easy Way*, gives very clear explanations and examples and is a great supplement to help the teen independently study math. It is from Barron's Educational Series.

CHAPTER 13

At Home with Science

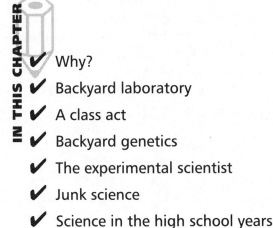

Exploring science can be a lot of fun, for both parents and children, even if you feel this is an area you are weak in. If this is the case, be willing to learn right alongside your children as they explore the vast machinations of physics, the wonders of the universe, and the secrets of the microscopic world.

Many questions young children ask can be a springboard into a science lesson, from why lights go on when you flip a switch, to why you add yeast to bread in order to make it rise. If you don't know the answers yourself, you will most likely learn while discovering this together.

When it comes to a formal study of science, you can still be playful. Exploit your children's sense of wonder and curiosity when looking at the world scientifically. If you do the following, you will see your children begin to take the lead when it comes to learning science—merely because they follow their own interests.

Why?

Learn to play upon your children's natural curiosity. If you're taking a walk on a lovely fall day, and your children decide to collect pinecones or leaves for an art project, talk about *why* the leaves or pinecones are on the ground. Explain the cycle of the seasons, and take a closer look at the signs around you. If you find a nest, talk about the need for shelter and discuss animal shelters from bird's nests (and what birds do when the weather turns) to the caves in which brown bears find shelter—and where they hibernate. You will note that if you keep asking "Why?" the topics expand. Why do animals need shelter? Why do birds fly south for the winter? Why do bears hibernate? You will realize you can't run out of things to explore or question, and once you cultivate this habit, science lessons will happen naturally.

Backyard Laboratory

Your own backyard is the furthest your young child has to venture for a wonderful laboratory experience. Have your children bring a magnifying glass into the yard, and observe small creatures together or examine the leaves of plants or blades of grass. Have them watch ants as they work carrying particles of food back to their hill, and explain how ants work together. You can easily explore this further by supplementing your lessons with books found at the library or by looking in an encyclopedia or on the Internet.

You may also want to consider planting a garden together. That would allow you to observe the life cycle of a plant and how this is exploited to feed our families. Children of any age can find a sense of satisfaction in nurturing the growth of a seedling into a full-grown plant that they can harvest to help feed the family. Make the experience exciting by bringing your produce into the house to use in a yummy kitchen chemistry project, to turn into jam, or for some other home economics project.

A Class Act

Encourage your children to learn about nature by observing creatures such as birds, bees, and butterflies. Each creature belongs to a group by which it is classified. This classification is part of the foundation of science. Explain that scientists classify different things according to common features or behaviors. You can use a book on tree, plant, or butterfly identification to help your children learn to look for the different commonalities or differentiations between these items of nature. Soon your children will begin looking at the world the way a scientist would, at least to some degree, and will better prepare themselves for more advanced science later on.

Backyard Genetics

If you have older children, your backyard can become a veritable genetics lab. Have your children read the works of Mendel, and then encourage them to learn about genetics firsthand. They can grow bean plants and log the results. Encourage them to study the different combinations that result from cross-germination, or, if you have the space, resources, and inclination, allow your children to breed an animal, such as a rabbit, to see the results, earning a profit along the way (contact local pet stores first, to see if this is a viable option!).

The Experimental Scientist

As your children grow more interested in science, you will want to begin directing them in experiments. You can typically find a wide assortment of simple home experiment books in your library, as well as many experiments you can conduct in your home posted on the Internet. Oftentimes these require nothing more than things you typically have in your cupboards or can purchase in your supermarket or local pharmacy. You can add to the atmosphere, however, by purchasing at least a few test tubes and petri dishes, which can be found through catalog science supply companies or in kits at your local toy store.

Prepackaged Kits

You may want to take advantage of the convenience of a prepackaged science set, though. Many parents remember the chemistry sets of their youth, and as was the case back then, they are still readily available today at your local toy shop, museum, or science supply store. In addition to traditional chemistry sets, however, there is now a vast array of mini-science kits available from companies such as Wild Goose or Minilabs Science. These kits typically range in price from about $5 to $25 and contain just about everything you need to perform the experiments they propose. For example, Minilabs sells a solar energy lab kit that contains a solar energy collector, solar heater, energy-focusing lens and thermometer, and a booklet that guides your children through more than 25 experiments, and we purchased it for $10. This is only one of many kits they sell, so you may want to look into their product line.

Wild Goose Company markets products such as Crash and Burn Chemistry or Newton's Body Shop. Newton's Body Shop is not for the faint of heart, though! The set teaches a good deal of anatomy. Your child can use it to build working models of eyes, ears, lungs, and it includes items such as ping pong balls, elastic cords, pipette cleaners, dowels, modeling clay, mirror, light bulb and socket, alligator clips, wire, candle, latex gloves, convex lens, pH paper, pipettes, plastic tubing, test tubes, acetic acid, sodium chloride, an instruction booklet, and a sheep's eye. And that's the short list! Yes, folks, we said a sheep's eye, as in a real one for you to examine! A set such as this retails for less than $25 and includes virtually everything you need to perform the experiments.

Be forewarned that the quality level of different kits can vary widely, and while most typically contain equipment to perform all the experiments contained within them, they may not necessarily be of the quality to build a home lab, since many are designed for one or merely a few uses. However, if you are looking for a fun, all-inclusive group of activities, you can't beat some of these premade kits! Brandon and Chris have used these fairly regularly, and we find that one kit typically can last a few weeks to a few months of a unit study, especially if you include a research component. Send your children to the library or the Internet to research the topic further, and you'll have a dynamite unit study.

Strutting Their Stuff

Encourage your children to share their knowledge. It helps reinforce what they've learned and helps get them accustomed to making presentations. Laura does a mini–family science fair when her boys complete one of these kits, sharing the newfound knowledge and demonstrating experiments to friends or family members. This is usually informal and sometimes happens spontaneously when eager children can't wait to show a friend "how cool it is to use the solar generator to heat this up."

Junk Science

Laura's boys love doing what they call "junk science." They stumbled upon this gem of a learning experience by accident one day, though Laura works hard to re-create it whenever possible now that she's learned how much the kids benefit from it. This is not the substandard science known by that term in professional circles, but instead it involves literally using junk to understand scientific principles.

Don't worry, this is not a difficult task. It is simply allowing your children to take apart junk such as broken electronics items to see how they are put together, or, in the case of that old clock, to see what makes it tick. Before you toss something, pause and determine whether or not this is something your kids would enjoy taking apart. You may want to get a simple children's book, such as one of those by Gail Gibbons, to help your children identify what it is they are looking at. Another great source is the book *How Things Work*. If you can't locate either of these, ask your children's librarian what she would recommend.

Be forewarned, though, while this is typically safe, you must first evaluate your children's abilities and set some ground rules. Perhaps the most obvious rule is that you don't plug in the object. Even if the object seems dead (broken beyond repair!), one never knows. Maybe John or Jessica will inadvertently repair it. Seriously, this has happened to Laura. Her son brought a toaster back to life when he unwittingly tightened a loose connection. Not only did he feel very accomplished, but he was able to see the intrinsic value in taking a closer look at things before giving up on them—a lesson that is applicable in many areas of his life.

Does junk science appeal to you? While giving your children a broken toaster or radio to pull apart before tossing it out may not be such a bad idea, it may at first seem a little misdirected or out of place. You may wonder how you can apply this to a current science topic you are studying. Well, you may not be able to immediately. Perhaps you will put it aside for a later date and create a unit study around it. Or you may decide to take a "break day" from your current topic of study and focus on this for a day or two.

This is a great time to teach your children about radio waves, transistors, or how things work in general, by taking advantage of an opportunity such as a broken radio. So be willing to consider allowing the flexibility of embracing such opportunities as they occur or at least being prepared to take them on at the next chance you get.

Okay, we've sold you on the potential of junk science, but perhaps you are fortunate enough to not have things breaking down around you? Try scoping out yard sales, thrift shops, and your neighbors' basements (ask first, of course!) for such items. This will typically cost you almost nothing and perhaps will even garner a working model for your child to enjoy.

However, be careful. Some electronic items store power, such as an old television that has a tube in it. These can still pack quite an electrical punch, and you will want to learn whether there is likely to be energy stored in there before you allow your children to fiddle with it. Again, this is where a good book or website comes in handy, as does a friend or family member who has experience with such items. It is terrific to give your children the opportunity to learn and explore in this hands-on way, but teach them to always put safety first and to act judiciously. Train your children to understand that if they aren't sure, they are better off being safe than sorry—find out before you touch anything questionable!

Science in the High School Years

If you've done the above, your child should already have a vast knowledge of scientific principles learned both hands-on and through nonfiction books. You can continue this approach throughout the high school years; however, if your children plan on attending college, you will want to incorporate a more specific science curriculum into your school days.

Typically students are expected to have had some biology, earth science, chemistry, and possibly physics prior to college. You can purchase textbooks for these subjects or look in science catalogs for full curricula that include lab components as well. Or you may want to see if your children can enroll in a remedial college course in any of these subject areas during their high school years, as college remedial courses are similar to what is taught in the high school years.

Some homeschool support groups hire a teacher to instruct a group of students in a particular area of science, which allows a number of children to formally study a subject at a highly reduced rate. However, you don't have to go this far if your children will follow textbooks and home lab directions.

If your children struggle with one particular subject, you may want first to try a different textbook—some science textbooks are far clearer than others. You also may want to get a book from the library that may cover a specific topic in a clearer way. For instance, if your children seem to be doing well in biology, but suddenly don't "get" the respiratory system, you may want to find a book on the respiratory system in your library. It may be that another author can explain the concept more simply than the original textbook did.

Keep in mind that there are terrific software programs that can supplement your science courses and more Internet websites than you can imagine. You can even find virtual frog dissection options to round out a biology course, if you so wish. You can also purchase home dissection kits, if you prefer. When it comes to chemistry, you can purchase a monopoly-like game called Elemento, which teaches your children the periodic table of the elements while they play. These are just a few of the many options out there. The thing to keep in mind is that there *are* a wide variety of options that you can explore, and teaching science to your high school–aged homeschooler doesn't have to be complicated or boring.

CHAPTER 14

At Home with Social Studies

Many people remember social studies class as boring and tedious. However, if you were blessed with a teacher who had a gift for making history come alive, your perspective is likely to be very different. You can master the art of bringing history alive for your children in just that way with just a little effort on your part. Begin by having lots of conversations with your children about different historical facts, famous people, and events. Sure, you can use a textbook to guide you, or as many prefer, a combination of overview books and biographies that cover specific periods of time, events, movements, or historical figures. You can also visit history museums and reenactments or incorporate programming on the History Channel into your social studies lessons. Add Internet resources to your arsenal of tools and you'll have a wide variety of ways to bring history alive for your children, making lessons and discussions far more memorable.

Before you begin planning social studies activities, though, you will want to first examine precisely what social studies covers. Social studies is a catch-all title given to the study of topics that include peoples, places, and events throughout the course of time. However, that is only the foundation, since social studies includes the study of geography, political science, civics, and citizenship, as well. The ultimate goal is to help the student understand how decisions and events of the past have helped shape the world today—and from there, to realize that the decisions and events of the present will help shape the world of tomorrow.

Clearly one can see why studying people, places, and events of the past are necessary, but sometimes it is not so clear as to why the other topics are important. Geography and political science are taught to help one understand not only *where* events occurred, but *why*. Geographic location, when coupled with specific political beliefs, can create a subtle (and sometimes not-so-subtle) interplay that can move peoples and nations to actions they might otherwise not have considered—and these actions can have drastic consequences on the very shape of the geo-political world. For this reason, it is necessary to study these topics in order to grasp historical information in the clearest context.

Finally, civics and citizenship are added to the mix to help students grow into responsible citizens who can successfully participate in the community and ultimately the world at large. Hopefully, they will be prepared to do exactly that, having spent their school years studying the wide range of topics covered by social studies. So as you can see, the hodgepodge of topics that makes up social studies actually is cohesive and not merely a bunch of topics lumped together in one category. So, while it is a broad area of study, it is an important one. And do not fear—it is one that you can impart to your children in a way where they will truly grasp its importance. Read on to get some ideas as to how to do just this!

History in Everyday Life

Laura found that she could turn daily conversations, be they about current events or grandma's memories, into history lessons! First, though, she taught the boys that each moment we live soon becomes part of our own personal history and that history itself constantly evolves over the course of our day-to-day living. While this might initially sound drastic, if you think about it you will see how this is true.

Once Laura's boys understood that their own lives had a history attached to them, she explored their personal history with them. This usually happened at the dining room table. Over breakfast she might describe the day Brandon was born, which was a very amusing tale since she had gone into labor during a family reunion. The result was a hospital filled with family members. Nurses claimed they broke all hospital records for the number of visitors at a child's birth. Christopher then heard of his own dramatic entry into the world, seven weeks prematurely. The boys loved hearing of their own stories, listening breathlessly to what happened to the premature Chris or laughing hilariously about how relatives argued over who would get closer to the nursery window to peer at the new family member first.

This was just the beginning of learning about personal history. Several months were spent learning about past family events that helped establish the world they moved in daily. With each passing month, the boys gained a clearer understanding of their prememory childhood years, and soon they were asking relatives about their childhoods as well. Soon they were driven to document the information, so they filled scrapbooks with photographs, drawings, and written accounts of events. They were creating "History of Me" books. This was their first introduction to a history book. What it did was put into perspective for them that history is about real people who were once real children and who belonged to real families.

"Real" World History

Of course, soon they were learning the history of an increasingly larger world. Stories of aunts and uncles, grandparents, and family friends sparked further curiosity, and they soon saw a picture of life as others lived it. They learned that others carried with them wartime memories, and that while a great uncle was fighting World War II, aunts and family friends were fighting in their own way back home and doing their part to help in the war effort.

This opened the door to learning more about those historical events. What caused World War II? Did others view it as their relatives did? What was it like for people in other parts of the world?

As you can see, Laura's boys don't view history as a boring subject to be learned, but as a fascinating process of understanding the world as experienced by those in the past. From there it all continues to expand. Soon they wonder, "Wow, if grandma felt this, I wonder what *her* mother felt?" This leads to a curiosity about different times, places, cultures, and events throughout history—which now seems alive.

A Caveat

Kids can ask some pretty heavy-hitting questions, and if you encourage your children to look closely at the world around them and to compare and contrast issues both past and present, sometimes you may find yourself having to answer questions that aren't always easy for adults to answer. You may field questions such as, "Why do people kill one another in wars?" "Why do people protesting for peace sometimes use violence themselves?" "Why are there people starving in the world, when others have so much that it spoils?"

Our suggestion, if you find this to be the case, is to answer as honestly as possible, even if this means admitting that you don't really understand it either. Then perhaps suggest that you can investigate the situation further together to see what kind of answers you can come up with. Let your children learn that just as other people before them have affected the world in a "big" way, they can too if they put their minds to it—even when it comes to situations they don't quite understand. There is an important level of empowerment for children when learning that even small things they do can contribute to the solution of a bigger problem. So, keep your mind open and be ready to explore issues with your children. You'll find that not only are your children learning, but that sometimes they help you to grow as well.

Biography as History

Just as your children's interests will be piqued by the stories of those they know, they may just be inspired by reading stories of others as well. Biographies can be a fascinating way to learn history and to get a healthy dose of character education along with it.

Reading accounts of the past from the perspective of the person who experienced it can provide a much clearer understanding of the time. It can be personally inspirational, too. As a child Laura read a book about Rachel Carson and believed maybe she too could change the world if she studied hard and learned to write well. Her boys have had similar responses to biographies, finding inspiration from those who came before them, especially when they discovered similarities between their own childhood and those of people who grew up to do great things. It puts things into perspective to realize that even George Washington, Martin Luther King, Jr., and Wynton Marsalis were at one time just regular little boys. With this in mind, consider encouraging your children to read biographies. Not just those of past presidents, Harriet Tubman, or Neil Armstrong (but by all means encourage them to read those too!), but also books about "smaller heroes," the people who have changed their communities or overcome great adversity.

If you incorporate biography into your history or social studies program, you may find that your children develop a more optimistic view of life. Many successful individuals had to overcome tremendous roadblocks on their way to success and exhibited strong examples of good character traits, such as perseverance, honesty, strong work ethic, strength, kindness, and generosity.

Character Throughout History

If your children are reading (or watching) biographies or studying a particular event, don't miss the opportunity to do some character education at the same time you're learning about another topic. First, find out if the subject of the biography exhibited a particular tenacity or had to overcome unusual adversity. Then help your child recognize patterns of positive characteristics. Your goal need not be, "I want Johnny to be president of the United States someday," but "I want Johnny to be confident and to know his values clearly." Help him learn to discern these traits when he sees them in others. Ask him questions such as, "What seems to have motivated Sosa to break the home run record?" "Do you think it was merely that he was good at the game, or do you think there was something going on in his mind that helped him accomplish this?" "Were there times where he felt pressured or wanted to quit?"

Do this in a conversational tone of interest and curiosity, not as a quiz on comprehension. You will accomplish several things this way: You will get a clear idea as to whether your children are indeed following up on reading assignments; you can gauge comprehension; and perhaps more important, you may learn something interesting yourself while enjoying a conversation with your children that strengthens bonds and helps them learn valuable character traits at the same time. Your children will likely come to see that you are genuinely interested in their opinions. This is all good stuff!

Covering It All

While encouraging your children to read biographies and overviews, you may want to add some structure to their pursuits. Perhaps this year you will study U.S. history or ancient civilizations. Next year may be the year of the inventors or the renaissance. This structure can help you tie things together better, especially if you begin by having your children read a survey of the topic, then encourage them to follow up with biographies and more specialized books in that subject area. You will find this to be a simple way to structure social studies so as not to miss things along the way, while still finding you have the freedom to enjoy a wide variety of works.

Where in the World?

To teach your children geography, develop a habit of using your map to find locations you hear or read about. Laura posted a giant wall map on her dining room wall, low enough for even the smallest kids to see it clearly. She then encouraged everyone to find every place they heard of, be it the setting of a novel, the city an international news story occurred in, or a country a friend recently traveled to. Then she had the children trace a path from their home to the destination, so that they got a clear understanding of how far away it is.

If you want to reinforce things learned on a map, try using a marker to outline cities, states, or countries you study, or perhaps add notes about their imports, their exports, or important events that took place there.

Help your child develop a habit of finding "where in the world things are," and you will discover that soon they will feel compelled to do this on their own—and soon enough geography will be learned somewhat effortlessly.

If you prefer a more structured approach to studying geography, there are plenty of products on the market to assist you, from workbooks to CD-Roms to board games. The Carmen San Diego geography games are particularly popular among the children we know; you can buy it as a board game or CD-Rom, and there is even a Web-based version.

You can also create your own version of the Carmen San Diego Web-based game by simply providing your children with clues and having them do the "detective" work to figure out which location you are talking about. For instance, they may need to look up which country produces oil in large amounts, was under an embargo in 1994, and is located in the Gulf. Encourage them to use the Internet, encyclopedias, and history books to try and solve the mystery based on the clues you provide.

This method can be used first to teach the 50 states, as well as their territories and, eventually, the entire world.

When studying the United States, state book projects are very popular among the homeschoolers we know. It can be time consuming, and many opt to stretch it out across several years, but it isn't a difficult project and can be a lot of fun.

Have your children study one state at a time, entering the information they gather into the binder. Have them first trace the outline of the state, the flag, the bird, flower, and so forth, and color them in. Have them take notes on any information they learn. You can determine what you want to focus on, but make sure to include the state capital, major cities, rivers, and mountain areas, population, major imports and exports, and what it is most famous for. On the first page for each state, list the basic information, and on the following pages have your children log anything that piqued their interest. One family we know draws a picture of the state license plate on the front page of each state section, and watches for them on vehicles when they are out and about.

This project can be as involved or as simple as you would like it to be. Most of the information could be quickly gathered from an encyclopedia entry, from a "state book" or a book about the United States, or one of many Internet websites. However, some families encourage their children to write to the state's chamber of commerce or visitor's center for information, and they accumulate all kinds of interesting, oftentimes colorful and attractive, literature to add to their state pages. Additionally, their children get the benefit of becoming accustomed to writing to places for information. We know of a family that takes this a step further, having their children plan an imaginary vacation to the state, using a U.S. map to find out how they could drive there and plotting out their itinerary using the information they received during research. Once a year they actually make a trip based upon their research—a wonderful reward for hard work, as well as inspiration for future projects!

Now that's really bringing social studies to life!

CHAPTER 15

At Home with Foreign Language

There are many ways that homeschooled kids can acquire the ability to speak in a foreign language. Some public school systems will allow homeschooled students to take foreign language courses along with the school's students, and some private schools also offer this service. There are often other options for classroom learning which vary according to the community in which you live. Or you might decide to hire a tutor to teach you and your kids a language. However, for the die-hard home-schooling do-it-yourselfer, there are also plenty of options.

If you know a foreign language, you are in a good position to get your children started in language learning, but it's not essential. You will, however, need to find a way for the children to regularly hear the language spoken by a native speaker and practice speaking in the language. There are audiotapes and CDs, computer programs, and tutors that can fill this need. Ideally, you can learn the language along with your children so that all of you can practice conversing. You may be intimidated by the prospect of memorizing verb conjugations and vocabulary lists as many us of did in high school, but learning a foreign language can be fun if you go about it in a playful way.

Choosing a Language

For some of you this will be an easy decision because you will naturally opt to teach a language in which you possess some proficiency, or one which is spoken by your children's relatives. For others the choice may not be so easy. You may choose from among the more commonly studied languages, such as Spanish, German, French, Latin, or perhaps Russian, Japanese or Chinese, but there are other options, as well. A number of homeschooling families choose to study American Sign Language in place of, or in addition to, a foreign language. With ASL you don't have to worry about pronunciations, but simply learn the signs by using videos, workbooks, or textbooks that teach ASL.

If your children are eager to learn a particular language, you may want to help them pursue it, since enthusiasm tends to lend itself to learning, even if you aren't sure that language will have much practical value. People who enjoy learning one language often go on to learn others, and foreign language study of any kind has its own rewards for those who are so inclined. You could always introduce a second more practical foreign language, such as Spanish, at some later date if you see the need.

Starting Early

You may want to consider preparing your children for language studies long before you begin formal classes. We all know that young children in bilingual homes seem to learn both languages easily. During the early years, the human brain is exquisitely primed for learning spoken language, and homeschooling parents may want to take advantage of this. Some people find bilingual play groups, either formally organized ones or impromptu on playgrounds where foreign kids come to play. If you live in a metropolitan area, you may well have friends, neighbors, or business associates who have bilingual children who might be potential playmates for your children.

If getting your children to interact with kids whose first language isn't English is not practical in your situation, there are other ways you can introduce them to the chosen language. You can have them watch videos designed for this purpose, such as the Early Advantage videos or Bilingual Baby, and have them listen to audio resources such as the Storybridges or Teach Me series. When your children are able to use a computer, you could have them play some foreign language games for children. (You will find these in stores with good selections of educational software for kids.) There are many colorful entertaining word books that you can read to your young children, providing that you know how to pronounce the words. If you browse in bookstores, homeschooling websites, or catalogues, you will find many products that you can use with your young children to teach common words and phrases of the language you've chosen to introduce. There are also more complete foreign language programs for young children, like Power Glide's children's courses.

There are a number of foreign language programs for older elementary-aged kids and high school students. There are computer programs such as the Language Now! Series, Triple Play! Plus series, and others which use a variety of interactive activities to teach a language. When shopping for software for foreign language software, note whether it includes a mechanism for having the learner practice repeating what he hears. Some kids will learn a lot of vocabulary and grammar from playing the games, but don't speak when they are supposed to and never get that practice. If you have that sort of child, you might need to find other ways to get her using her foreign language knowledge to converse. You can enhance your child's foreign language learning by making it a game.

In addition to the rapidly growing selection of software providing foreign language instruction, there are a number of more traditional text-based programs which use audiotapes or CDs to allow the learner to hear native speakers of the language during the lessons. Many of the independent study programs will allow children to enroll in its foreign language courses without enrolling in the rest of the program. There are also programs using texts, workbooks, and audio recordings that can be purchased for homeschooling use, such as the Power Glide programs.

Playful Things to Do

There are also ways in which to make learning a foreign language a lot of fun. You could try some of the following in your home to create a playful atmosphere for learning:

- **You could announce to your young children that the language they are learning is a secret code and only those who can crack the code can understand you.** Then at meal time, give them chances to show off their superior knowledge by saying things such as, "Johnny, please pass el pan," or "Would you rather have leche o agua?"

- **Have a foreign vocabulary scavenger hunt.** Hide a number of objects, for example, a pencil, apple, rock, and hat, and make a list (using foreign words, of course) for each child so that each has the same number of objects to find. The object of the game is for each child to find all the objects on her list. If she can't remember what one of the words means, she can ask you for hints, but will lose a little speed that way. Each child can win a prize.

- **Present your children with a series of simple instructions written in the language they are learning.** Set it up so that following the instructions correctly brings the child to a goal, for example, instruct him to put on his shoes and jacket, get his allowance money, and go out to the blue car, sit in the back seat, and buckle his seat belt. Then you can take him on a trip to the local ice cream parlor or toy store.

- **Announce that tonight at dinner you will speak nothing but Spanish, or whichever language your children are learning.** This works well if you do it after they have learned quite a bit of meal-related vocabulary and phrases. If you want to add an element of competition in a family with several older kids, you might offer a prize to the one who participates most actively.

These are just a few of the many, many ways in which you can teach foreign language. Just because you aren't proficient at speaking a foreign language doesn't mean it has to be difficult to teach it. Just embrace the challenge and make a commitment to yourself that you're going to have fun doing it, and then take the first step.

As with mathematics or any subject you are teaching, attitude can go a long way in paving a smooth road for learning. Instead of being intimidated by the prospect of learning a new language, dive into it with the attitude that it's going to be a lot of fun. One of the easiest ways to mas-

ASL Fun for Kids

Young children especially like this option since they can send messages to one another across a playground, completely stumping those around them who are not "in the know." My children have been studying ASL in addition to our primary foreign language programs, and it is interesting to see them take the opportunity to watch an interpreter on a television show.

ter a language, if you don't grow up in a family that speaks the language, is to immerse yourself in it. In theory, one of the best ways to learn Italian would be to live and go to school (or work) in Italy, seconded by living with an Italian relative that speaks the language as a native or at least by spending a large amount of time with that person. This level of immersion makes one feel it necessary to pick up the language in order to survive, or at least in order to communicate thoughts, needs, and wants to the largest variety of people.

If you *do* speak a second language, teach your children some vocabulary words in the other language as they are growing up and learning English. It is much easier for children to learn at a younger age.

CHAPTER 16

At Home with Art

Expose your children to the many different art mediums and let them create! This is the simplest introduction to art. Most children have experience with crayons and markers by the time they reach kindergarten age, but you can provide a variety of other materials they can use to create their own works of art. The younger set will also enjoy activities such as finger painting, collage making, and working with soft play clay. Older children can experiment with other mediums such as oil pastels, paints ranging from watercolors to tempera to oils, or clay and papier-mâché. Your lessons in other school subjects can incorporate hands-on activities and the study of art history and the various styles of art. Here are some ways you might include art in the study of other subjects.

- **Have your children draw or paint or sculpt something related to what you are reading aloud at the time.** They might paint a rainbow while you read to them about how rainbows are made.

- **Have your children create a work of art that is related to a general topic they've been learning about.** If you're teaching your children about Pilgrims, you can have them make papier-mâché turkeys, draw a picture of the first Thanksgiving, or sculpt a three-dimensional Thanksgiving scene from clay.

- **Have your children draw or paint illustrations for a story they write.**

- **Study the art of the period of history that your children are currently studying.** If they are learning about ancient civilizations, show them pictures of ancient art or take them to see pieces in a museum.

Are you learning about a famous scientist or explorer? Is there a painting of that person? Not only look at the painting, but learn a little bit about the artist at the same time, and your child will naturally gain an education in art history, even if you don't dedicate a specified study period for it each day.

Have your children draw a diagram and label the parts of something you are teaching them in science; for example, draw a cell and label its cell wall, nucleus, and the like.

Art History and Appreciation

There are many resources for helping your children develop an appreciation for various styles of art. Here are some ideas:

- **Browse through "art appreciation" books for children.** Read the captions together and discuss what you see.

- **Visit art museums.** Guided tours are usually very interesting and informative.

- **Browse in the gift shops in art museums for hands-on activities involving art.** They often sell things such as jigsaw puzzles of famous paintings, postcards of famous works, as well as beautiful art books. If you don't have a museum close by, take a virtual tour of one on the Internet.

- **Read books about great artists and their work.** Good resources for this purpose include Mike Venezia's *Getting to Know the World's Greatest Artists* Series, and Mila Boutan's *The Art Activity Pack* Series.

Focused Art Study

If your children have developed art skills and are ready for more methodical instruction, there are wonderful products to assist you. Visit your local art store and ask about self-teaching art kits and videos. Check out an assortment of how-to books on drawing from your public library or purchase one or more from a bookstore or art store. If you have a child with a particular interest in art, you might want to find him an art class that will help him develop his skills further.

In addition to the ones with which most of us are most familiar, such as drawing or painting, there are many more forms of artistic expression. So if your children take an interest in one of them, you can help them track down books and other sources of information about it. Laura's boys adore special effects art, and she has friends who work in this field that have allowed them a look at their work. Even if she didn't have friends in the field, there are ways that she could nurture her children's interest in it. There are good books on the subject, websites, biographies of top special effects artists, and magazines and television shows dedicated to this topic.

While learning about special effects art, the boys have amassed knowledge of digital imaging, computer animation, traditional animation, and all sorts of art mediums such as paint, resins, and sculpey clay. Their enthusiasm for the topic prompted them to learn from many different areas of knowledge, because they found that there were things they needed to learn in order to understand the special effects business. Suddenly they were writing skits, creating scripts, making storyboards, doing all kinds of design work, operating a video camera, and so forth. This project eventually covered almost every subject.

Our 10 Favorite Art Tools

1. Butcher Block Paper. With a huge roll of butcher block paper, found in a warehouse store or restaurant supply store, you have the ability to give your children as large or small a work space as necessary. Additionally, you can cover a table with it at a kids' dinner party, and allow your guests to get creative. We've also hung 4-foot spans up on our wall at birthday parties and allowed all the guests to write birthday messages or draw pictures on them, providing a unique souvenir for the birthday child. But this is only the beginning! Think how encouraging it is for your children to know their ideas are not limited to the size of a small piece of paper. Feel free to cover a large expanse of wall and to let them get creative. It is a freeing experience that encourages children to create. And if you have toddlers, these are great ways to keep your walls free of scribbles—well, at least they are easier to remove!

2. Markers, Crayons, and Colored Pencils. These are some basics that every homeschool should try to acquire. You can find inexpensive ones, but if you have a serious artist for a student, you can find high-quality ones in art supply stores. We like the Berol Prismacolor pencils because their colors are so rich and they blend very well.

3. Sculpey Clay. Sculpey clay is one of the most popular art materials in Laura's home. This is a professional art clay which is more costly than basic clay, but worth every penny. Your children can make sculptures and then bake them in your oven to harden them. It comes in basic white and a variety of colors, including some neon ones. Additionally, you can buy rolls of sculpey already pressed into a pattern that you can slice (like slice-and-bake cookies!) and bake to make into necklaces, earrings, etc. Additionally, now there are sculpey clay guns (reminiscent of Play-Doh guns), pattern makers, and so on. This is a wonderful medium, and you may want to try it yourself.

4. Recipe Clay. For the beginning sculptor or for an afternoon of great fun, nothing beats homemade clay. You can make wonderful ornaments for your home, and have a great time learning all about sculpture. The recipe is simple enough to make: Mix together 1 cup all-purpose flour and ½ cup salt. Mix in ½ cup warm water, and knead it to blend thoroughly.

To color the clay, add a few drops of food coloring and knead until color is evenly distributed. It can be stored in an airtight container for about a week. Sculptured pieces can be allowed to air dry, and thin ones can be baked at 200 degrees for about two hours.

5. Paint. Now here is a broad category. For younger children you can start with something simple like tempera paints. These are cheap, clean up easily, and are relatively easy to find. Add an inexpensive plastic palette and a few different sizes of paint brushes and your children will likely be inspired. Watercolor paint is another option most children enjoy, and, of course, young children love getting their hands into finger paints. If your young artist is ready for another medium, you can have him try the costlier acrylic or oil paints.

6. Oil Pastels. Like crayons in some ways, these are far richer and are fun to experiment with. The rich colors expand your children's creative options, and they will enjoy this foray into imaginative use of color and texture. They are a bit messier than crayons, so be forewarned. You can find inexpensive versions, but the more expensive ones you purchase from an art supply store tend to give better results.

7. Craft Box. This is a catch-all box filled with remnants of fabric, wallpaper, scraps, items like empty paper towel rolls, scraps of foil, pinecones, glitter, ribbon, yarn scraps, or any other odds and ends your children may want to use in future art projects. Keep the box filled by getting creative—before you discard things, see if you can envision it being inspiration for a child's art project. Laura began by filling one with art basics—glue sticks, tape, kid-safe scissors, paste, pens, markers, pencils, crayons, and a few rulers. From there it kept growing— fabric scraps from last year's Halloween costume, glitter from decorated pinecones, stencils from an Easter egg decorating kit, and leftover wallpaper all went in there, as well as large scraps of construction paper that remained after we made a variety of projects. You may also want to include things such as pipe cleaners, craft sticks, Styrofoam balls, or anything else that strikes your fancy. Coffee cans can be used to organize things within the box. Give them some interesting odds and ends to work with, and watch your kids have hours of fun creating everything under the sun!

8. Smocks. Smocks make art time more relaxed for both parent and children since no one has to worry much about ruining clothing. Make sure you have at least one smock for every artist in your family. For children, an old shirt of mom or dad's, preferably one that buttons down the front, works well. They are easier to slip in and out of when they're covered with paint than a pullover shirt, and kids enjoy wearing the grown up item.

9. Designated Project Area. If your home is large enough, set aside an area as a designated project area. This need not be used simply for art class, but for science projects, mixing batters (your child doing so), making holiday gifts, building models, putting together puzzles—any kind of work in progress that can get messy. You need not have an entire room to set aside, but merely a corner. Your goal should be to make it mess friendly. If it is carpeted, lay down a floor covering. You can buy a premade plastic mat or use a flannel-backed plastic tablecloth or inexpensive shower curtain to keep your floor free from spills. Place an old table in the area or cover one with butcher paper after each cleanup so it is ready for the next project. Add some shelves or a cabinet to store supplies and perhaps some stools or chairs, and you are set to go. If you cannot designate an area, keep supplies in one location in your kitchen. Make sure you have a table covering that is quick and easy to use and all your supplies are in one place so that they are readily available. Keeping things organized in this way encourages young children to do artwork often. It makes it easier to start a project when there is less chance to be frustrated by being unable to find supplies, and cleanup is routine and simple. It also makes messy projects easier on the parental mind—if you know the mess is containable and easy to clean up, you will find you are freer to encourage your child to expand his creative vision.

10. Books. These may be coloring books, how-to-draw books, craft books, and so on. Having things that inspire you to try new projects are worth their weight in gold. Teach your children that they can learn almost anything they want to know from a good instructional book. You can also just fill your area with books or artwork that is inspirational and in the vein in which you are trying to work.

Of course, there are many other things you'll want to round out your art supply arsenal—odds and ends like pencil sharpeners, wastebaskets, construction paper, and erasers. You may want to even add items such as a small easel or a drafting table. However, the top 10 list will give you a good start, and you can grow your arsenal from there, having better determined which products are in greatest demand with your brood. The bottom line is that if you provide ample materials and the freedom in which to explore comfortably with them, without worry as to mess, "accuracy," or preconceived notions, your little artists will indeed blossom. You may even find you have just as much fun sculpting candy cane ornaments as your children do—and maybe even more so.

At Home with Music

There are a number of ways to teach your children music. You could teach your children about rhythm, beats, rests, and other basic music concepts, along with a smattering of music appreciation, and leave it at that. If you are an especially musically inclined family, or if your children indicate an interest, you might facilitate their learning to play one or more musical instruments. Some parents want their children to learn to read music, regardless of whether they ever play a musical instrument, while others focus on exploring different types of music.

Introducing Your Children to Music

If you feel unsure of yourself in this, you can find all sorts of videos and CDs that have music and instructions for rhythm games you can play with your children. You may also want to purchase some simple instruments, such as a triangle, cymbal, or pennywhistle, and a beginning instruction book. A plastic recorder and introductory instruction booklet can be purchased for less than $10, or you can just pick up the plastic recorder and find an instruction book at your library.

Have fun with the process by making it into a game. When Laura's boys were younger, they played a game similar to "Mother May I." She would ask them to play a note, and if they played the correct note, they earned the right to take a giant step forward. This same game, incidentally, got used in their home for many different subjects. By the time they reached the "finish line" they would have played each of the notes. This same game works well if you hold up flash cards of musical notes as the children are learning them.

There are a number of ways children can be taught to read music. Traditionally, many music teachers will teach one note at a time as they are teaching the child to sing or play the note. Laura started out by telling her boys that she was going to teach them a secret code that they could use to write to one another. She explained that musicians used this code, and that if a person could break it, and learn a few things about an instrument, he could "talk" or make the instrument talk as he wanted it to. This project fascinated the little boys. She then went on to teach them to read music notes. Where there wasn't an alphabet letter, they would use a traditional alphabet letter, so the word "boot" would only have the letter "b" written in a musical note, followed by O-O-T. However, the word "CAB" would be spelled out all in musical notes. The challenge was then to make up sentences with words that could be spelled out completely in musical notes. Then she showed them how to play notes on the recorder and piano by reading them off a page.

Helping Your Children Learn to Play a Musical Instrument

There are many home music instruction opportunities, and if you explore your local library you can find books on learning almost any musical instrument. Many music stores or catalog sales companies carry a wide variety of materials for the self-taught musician, so begin exploring and see what you can find. There are many music CD-Roms or videos that teach your children how to play an instrument, step by step, even without your interaction. Some of the CD-Rom programs are interesting in that you connect a music keyboard via MIDI cables to the computer and actually play the piano keyboard along with the CD-

Rom lesson. Many children enjoy these economical alternatives to private music lessons and learn a lot through them. A serious musician, though, will probably wish to spend some time with a professional instructor. If you prefer, you may decide that teaching someone to play music is something you'd rather leave to a professional, and arrange for your children to take music lessons.

Music Appreciation

Where do you begin? Perhaps the easiest way to begin exploring music is simply to listen to it with your children. Listen to your favorite CDs and radio stations, and just share things you know with your children. When you listen to an unfamiliar genre of music, you can point it out to your children. If you'd like, dance or sing along from time to time. Young children usually love clapping games, so you might try clapping the rhythm along with them. Simply from listening to a variety of music with an interested adult, the children will learn quite a bit about different types of music and what helps classify them.

You can find some books in your library or bookstore that give more information about the types of music to which your children listen. The Dummies Books and Idiot's Guides put out books that explain the basics, such as the *Dummies Guide to Classical Music* or *Jazz for Idiots*, that help you understand anything you are unsure of so that you can better explain it to your children—and depending upon your children's ages, they can read the books themselves. These are by no means the only books on understanding music. Your local library and bookstores are filled with music appreciation books, and you can educate your children quite well through these. Additionally, many libraries have recordings you can borrow to expose your children to music you would otherwise not purchase.

Oftentimes you can find free or inexpensive opportunities for your children to view live music. Many bookstores, such as Borders or Barnes and Noble, have free concerts at different times throughout the year, where your child may see a quartet, a jazz band, or a classical guitarist. Many cities have "symphony in the park" events, where you can bring a lawn chair or blanket and listen to the symphony play under the stars for free or low-cost admission. During holiday seasons, many public places, such as shopping malls, have free entertainment by choral groups, bands, or solo musicians. Opportunities abound if you keep your eyes open for them.

There are some fascinating stories about the lives of many, many musicians, from Beethoven and Bach to Mozart and Marsalis. Delve into the shelves of your library, and don't overlook the obvious tie-ins between music and history. This is clear when discussing historical music, but don't overlook the music scene in the days of the Beatles or the days of grunge—they are equally important as Bach and Mozart were to their times, as music often reflects the times themselves. Additionally, have your children examine the music closely to see the story the music tells—yes, even instrumental music tells a story. Train your child to be receptive to the stories music shares, especially the music where it isn't spelled out in words. If you doubt music tells a story, listen for yourself to works like *Peter and the Wolf*, or *Bolero*, which was considered so seductive it has been used by Hollywood many times to indicate a steamy scene about to begin.

So, read to your children about the lives of the composers and what drove them to work on what they did, and follow up by listening.

Teaching Your Children to Recognize Instruments

- There are many books that teach your children to recognize the musical instruments by appearance, and some that even come with music CDs that teach them to recognize the sounds each instrument makes.

- You can also take advantage of outdoor performances at an event such as "Symphony in the Park" to point out to your children which instruments are making the different sounds as they hear them.

- Have your children listen to a recording that uses *Peter and the Wolf* to introduce the instruments' sounds for a fun lesson.

Many of us have friends and relatives who have musical instruments in their attics that they haven't played in years. Try persuading them to pull out their old bassoon or clarinet, and let your child hold it and hear how it sounds.

At Home with Physical Education

There are a variety of ways to handle physical education in the home-school setting. When designing your physical education program, keep in mind that a good one will help your children maintain at least a minimum level of fitness while developing their eye-hand coordination and establishing the habits of a healthy lifestyle. Such a program will benefit them well beyond their school years.

Your first step in this direction will be to determine how you will help your children do this. Your goals need to be specific to your family. For instance, if your family tends toward couch potato living, a worthy goal would be getting your children (preferably along with the rest of the family) to lead a more physically active lifestyle. If you're an active family your goal might be to have your children improve their game in a particular sport or learn a new skill set such as swimming, as opposed to basketball.

Your physical education program doesn't have to be modeled after the ones you may recall from your school days. Instead, focus on getting your children to consistently participate in a variety of active games, sports, exercises, and other activities that develop muscles while giving their cardiovascular systems a good workout.

Keep in mind, too, that regularity is the key to healthy living. Making the same good choices time and again, about exercising, eating, or choosing not to smoke or drink, helps create a healthy lifestyle. So, get your kids active, teach them to make good choices, and help them develop a healthy lifestyle that will remain with them for the rest of their lives. In the process, you will have achieved the goals of a physical education program.

Tips For Getting Active

Here are some ideas to get your children moving. See which ones might fit into your family's life.

- **Limit the amount of time your children spend watching television and videos and playing computer games.** Forcing them to choose alternatives to these sedentary pursuits may encourage them to pursue more physically challenging activities.

- **Make frequent excursions to a playground or park.** You can bring along a ball to roll, kick, toss, or throw, improving eye-hand coordination as well. If you do this during hours that most children are in school, you may even happen upon other homeschooling families.

- **When shopping for toys, choose ones that will encourage physical activity.** Instead of another video game, opt for a basketball hoop, baseball glove, soccer ball, tricycle, bicycle, roller skates, jump rope, or tennis racket.

- **Sign your children up for a local sports team.** Check to see what is offered in your community. You will likely be surprised at how inexpensive this option is.

- **Start each morning with a brief P.E. session to get everyone alert and ready for the day ahead.** If mom and dad participate as well, they'll be setting a positive example. You could come up with a routine of calisthenics to do every day or could have a variety of different routines and rotate them. Or you could simply go for a walk together.

- **Take walks with your children.** If you have several children, and walk with one, it will serve as both physical activity *and* one-on-one time with your child.

- **Incorporate hiking into your science class, and cover science and physical education at the same times.** Look for opportunities for movement and fitness that can be coupled with other educational experiences.

- **Buy aerobic videos that appeal to your children and work out together.**

- **Use videotapes to learn a new dance with your children, be it ballroom, salsa, or the Macarena.** Or, you can just put on music and dance.

- **Lead your young children through a silly exercise session in which they move rapidly through your home** hopping like bunnies, walking on all fours like bears, flying like bats, and doing any other animal movements you can come up with.

- **Encourage your children to pursue activities in which they compete against themselves (such as running or swimming), and keep records so they can work on surpassing their personal best.** You might time their swimming laps or running or count how many push-ups they can do. This way you can encourage your children to continue to stretch their abilities, without feeling they have to perform better than their siblings or friends.

- **Make sure your children learn how to play some of the sports other children their age tend to play.** If your children's friends start an impromptu game of basketball or football in someone's backyard, your children can join right in if they know how to play. This also holds true for activities such as jumping rope and roller skating.

- **Encourage active play dates.** If your children have a play date with a friend, encourage them to bike, roller skate, or play ball.

- **Keep extras of things such as baseball mitts and tennis rackets, so that visiting children can do these activities with your children.**

Organized Team Sports

Organized team sports can help round out a good home physical education program if you and your children are comfortable with them. They are a viable way to get exercise while enjoying oneself.

However, this is a personal decision. Some parents love team sports while others abhor them. While one can argue the pros and cons, regardless of whether or not your children ever participate in an organized team sport, you should at least teach them the basics of popular sports. Teach the rules of the game, so that they can be comfortable in social situations with their peers. Imagine how your children would feel if they're hanging out with a group of teens while the teens are discussing a football game they just watched if your children never heard of a touchdown before. While you may think this isn't important, it can't hurt to teach your children something new, so why not at least give them this social edge? You need not devote a lot of time to this. Watching sports on television or going out to watch an occasional ball game will at least give them some familiarity with these sports, even if they've never played.

However, actually playing the sport gives your children an even greater understanding, since they not only will become familiar with the sport, but again will get exercise as well. Playing on a team can also be beneficial in that your children will have to learn the nuances of working as part of a team, something homeschoolers don't always have an opportunity to learn in a typical family setting.

If you decide this is a good idea, there are likely to be many options in your area. Local governments typically have programs that provide a wide variety of opportunities to participate in team sports, often quite inexpensively. If there are a large number of homeschoolers in your area, you may even find that there is a homeschool intramural team. Churches oftentimes have sports programs as well.

When it comes to choosing a particular sport, you may simply want to sign your children up for the sports they are most passionate about. However, you may also want to consider other goals and choose a sport that focuses more on a particular skill development or one that seems to allow your children a greater variety of options for exploring their talents.

Ultimately, though, your goal should be that your children enjoy playing while learning some skills along the way. This way they will learn to see playing a game as yet another way to have fun while getting exercise and staying fit. As you can see, organized sports are certainly one way to meet physical education criteria; but remember, there are other ways to achieve this as well.

Health

Many traditional schools classify the subject of health under the umbrella of physical education. How you opt to teach health in your homeschool is your option. You can browse in libraries and bookstores where you will find all sorts of books about health-related topics, and there are also free government publications covering all sorts of substance abuse and sex education issues, as well as fitness and nutrition. Any of these materials can aid you in teaching health to your children. No matter what sort of information you decide is appropriate for your children at various stages, you will have no trouble finding materials to assist you.

You can cover a wide variety of topics. You may wish to include the following in your homeschooling health program.

- How to interpret nutritional information on food labels.
- Food groups and standard recommendations for eating a varied and balanced diet.
- The role of vitamins and minerals in our diets, and of fats, proteins, carbohydrates, and water.
- Planning and preparing nutritionally balanced meals.
- Health benefits of exercise.
- Accident prevention, including automobile safety issues and using protective gear when appropriate, such as bicycle helmets, electrical safety, and household hazards.
- Health issues related to substance abuse and strategies for avoiding harmful behaviors.
- Sexuality issues such as teen pregnancy and sexually transmitted diseases and reproductive health.
- Suicide and violence prevention.
- Topics found in the U.S. Department of Education's website, which offers a large number of free publications, including information to help parents talk with their children about drugs and other health issues: www.ed.gov.

Noncompetitive Games

If you want your children to play interactive games, but hate the idea of competition, you'll find there are plenty of books that provide ideas for

(*continued on page 130*)

(continued from page 129)
noncompetitive games for children. However, most childhood games can be modified so that they are no longer competitive. For instance, musical chairs can be played in a way that there are enough chairs for everyone, so that no one is "out" or so that if you are tapping the shoulder of someone sitting, you are fine. This enables children still to enjoy the pacing of the game, and to enjoy racing around to sit quickly, without having a competitive action. Additionally, tag-style games can be played in a manner in which the tagged person joins with the person who is "it," and the game is played until all players become a part of 'it.' Flex your creative muscle and think about how you can modify traditional games to delete the competitive element, and you will find that it doesn't have to be that difficult.

If you teach your children to exercise regularly, to eat nutritious, well-balanced meals, and to embrace a healthy lifestyle, you will be headed in the right direction. Consistency is an important part of achieving these goals, so make sure that your physical education program is not only fun but a regular part of life!

CHAPTER 19

School on the Run

✔ Every trip is a field trip

✔ Car time

✔ Vacationing

✔ Travel time tote

It's 9:00 Monday morning, and your preschooler is supposed to be coloring or playing with clay while you work with your first grader on reading and your fourth grader does math problems. Instead, your two older kids are squabbling about whose turn it is to sit in the front seat of the family van, and your little one is wailing because he's dropped his stuffed dinosaur in the cat's water dish. All three kids have dental appointments in 30 minutes, and you really ought to change out of your grape juice stained t-shirt.

So why are things not going as planned? Your carefully devised master schedule says nothing about sibling squabbles, wet dinosaurs, dental appointments, or grape juice spills. Many homeschooling books present models of intricately designed weekly schedules that look very professional on paper and help those of us who are insecure to feel more like "real" educators. Some people thrive on schedules, follow them faithfully, and can't imagine life without them. They want to know exactly what to expect at all times, and if they're lucky, their children share this preference.

The parent with this mindset probably would never have gotten into such a predicament anyway. He or she would have a van seating chart posted on the kitchen bulletin board, everyone would have climbed into the van a half hour earlier, the day's school plan would have been modified weeks in advance to accommodate dental appointments, and there would be plenty of time left to dry off the dinosaur and change the shirt. If this describes you, you may be tempted to skip this chapter, but please don't. Even the most meticulously organized homeschool will occasionally face an unavoidable disruption or two. Perhaps you wake up and find that your son has a 104 degree temperature, a burst pipe has flooded your entire downstairs, or the house is 90 degrees because the new air conditioning system has mysteriously gone on strike. There is no way you can avoid surprises such as this. However, you can take steps that prevent such situations from gobbling up all of your school time. Stay flexible, and be prepared to think outside the box when family business, vacations, or life's trials intrude on your homeschooling plan.

Every Trip Is a Field Trip

Most parents spend a substantial portion of their time shopping for necessities, ferrying kids to activities, waiting for car repairs, and running errands. Since these excursions sometimes prevent a homeschooling family from following its usual school day routine, it makes sense to be prepared to take advantage of educational opportunities that you may discover while you are out and about.

Many even mundane daily experiences can be fodder for a lesson. Let's take a look at some of the ways you can take advantage of learning opportunities as they arise.

Suppose your day is packed with errands to do that just can't be put off. You've got to fill up your gas tank before heading to the post office to mail a wedding gift to your nephew. From there, you'll proceed to the optometrist's office to pick up your contacts and to the pediatrician's office to pick up your daughter's soccer physical exam form. That is just the start of your day, though. Next, you plan on treating your mother to a birthday lunch at her favorite restaurant, and then an afternoon of shopping together, so you have time with mom, and get cleats for soccer, and groceries, too. You'll have just enough time to throw together a quick dinner before taking your daughter to her first soccer practice.

With such a full plate, you may be tempted to call off school for the day. While this is okay now and then, and if you stay in compliance with your state's requirements, it's a shame to spend a day off running errands. You'd much rather save that precious day off for something like a picnic at the park, a visit with friends, or a trip to the movies, but how can you possibly hold school today?

Guess what? You can, and it doesn't have to be difficult. First of all, while you are getting everything together, are there 20 minutes your child could spend doing a math lesson? If even that is too much to ask, don't worry, there are other ways to school on such days.

This is where "school on the run" comes in. Now, school on the run may not cover what you had planned on teaching today, but it can allow you to incorporate a good deal of learning into a day that could've wound up a wash otherwise.

Find five minutes to assess your situation. Try to do this the night before, if possible. If you don't already have a Travel Time Tote packed, fill a bag with any supplies you may need en route. If you do have a Travel Time Tote, take a minute to update it with current work, such as this week's spelling word list, the book you are reading together, and pens and pencils.

Once everyone's safely seat-belted into the car, think about your itinerary. Gas station first. On the way to the gas station, think of some questions to ask. Does your child know where gasoline comes from? If your child replies "the gas station," tell her a bit about fossil fuels, and just let the conversation go wherever it might lead. With older kids you can have a more sophisticated discussion about whatever seems most interesting at the moment. It could be gas prices, OPEC, supply and demand, air pollution, or anything at all that you can tie into a visit to the gas station.

If this seems less than inspiring, change the subject and find something else to talk about. You need not be an expert in any of the subjects you discuss. Just share whatever knowledge you have, and when time permits, you or a child can look up unanswered questions if so inclined.

While you're in line at the post office you can discuss the postal system: what postal workers do; why we use postage stamps; why we have zip codes; and how packages are weighed.

On the way to the optometrist's office, you can initiate a discussion with the older kids about what optometrists do. If your optometrist isn't busy, maybe she'd spend a moment explaining some aspect of her work to your children. If not, at least point out to them some of the equipment and any information you see in the office that may teach your children something about what optometrists do.

After lunch, you can assign one of the older children to add up the price of their meal, and figure out the tax and tip.

The supermarket presents plenty of opportunities for both younger and older kids to learn. There are things to count, colors to be identified, labels to be read, numbers to be manipulated, and much more. You might try giving a child tasks to do that reinforce concepts he or she is learning: You could say to a child who's learning the alphabet, "go over there to the cereal section and see if you can find a cereal that has an 's' on the front of the box." While weighing produce, you could take a moment to explain the process: "See, this scale lets me find out how heavy this bag of pears is. I want 4 pounds of pears. Do you see the 4-pound marking?" Another child might get to do a more complex task, such as weighing out 3¼ pounds of grapes. An older kid could use a calculator to figure out which brand of orange juice has the lowest price per ounce, or quart, or liter, or to keep a running total of the items you put in your cart. You can spend a couple of minutes explaining to him or her how to interpret the nutrition information on food labels, which could evolve into a discussion of food groups, vitamins, cholesterol, the role of the federal government in regulating food products, or any number of topics.

The ideas mentioned are just a few of the educational possibilities. Some of them may not appeal to you and your kids at all, but you can come up with many of your own that you can try with your children. All of these examples might be too much for one trip, or not enough.

If your kids (or you) are tired and distracted by the time you hit the post office, maybe it's time to take a break and listen to music or talk about the upcoming weekend's plans. Every moment of the day need not be filled with learning for it to be an effective school session. Your school day doesn't have to bear much resemblance to a traditional one for it to count. The above examples are only the tip of the iceberg. By using your ingenuity, you can incorporate learning into your errands and make every trip into a field trip.

Car Time

Most parents spend a considerable number of hours each week in the car, shopping, banking, ferrying kids to ballet lessons or baseball games. If you would like to take advantage of the captive audience in your vehicle, here are some suggestions.

- **Give an impromptu music appreciation lesson.** When a good jazz tune comes on the radio, for instance, you might say something like, "Hey kids! That guy playing the trumpet is Louie Armstrong. Have you heard of him?"

  If they respond with blank looks, you could say, "He was one of the best jazz soloists of the early 1900s! In jazz, there was usually a soloist who made up the music as he went along. That's called improvisation. You could discuss jazz until either your knowledge base or their patience runs out. You could do this with other kinds of music too.

- **Do some verbal drill work.** You can quiz a child on addition, subtraction, multiplication, or division problems, practice rounding numbers, estimating, finding factors, spelling words or Spanish vocabulary words, or drilling grammar concepts, among other things.

- **Have the children tell you about books they have been reading.**

- **Discuss current events.** If an interesting news story comes on the radio, you might comment on it.

- **Review something they've recently studied.** For example, have them practice picking out the prepositions from a sentence you make up.

- **Do health education.** This could involve discussing substance abuse, sex, mental illness, or any topics that are of particular relevance at the time.

Vacationing

One of the great things about homeschooling is that you don't necessarily have to take your family on vacations when everyone else does. Many state laws will allow homeschoolers to deviate from the public school calendar. So, if you wish, you can plan your trip to Disney World when the weather is relatively cool and the lines are short. If you're a family of avid skiers, you might prefer to have a long break from school in the winter rather than in the summer. If summers are miserably hot in your state, you might prefer to do schoolwork in your air-conditioned home all summer after taking an extra six weeks off during the beautiful spring months. You can arrange the school schedule to best suit your family.

If you want your school breaks to coincide with those of the local schools, you could plan to have school while on your vacation trip. Let's use a hypothetical trip to Florida as an example. A few weeks before the trip, you might browse through tourist information pamphlets, and look for fun, educational things to do in Florida. Maybe orange growers give tours. What museums are in the Orlando area? There's a medieval dinner theater that depicts knights competing in jousting tournaments while the audience feasts on medieval fare. Sea World and the Disney theme parks are packed with learning opportunities.

After you have a good idea of which activities you'll be doing, you could spend a few minutes in a library gathering together children's books relevant to your family's impending vacation. You might find books on whales and dolphins, alligators, sharks, knights, habitats, oceans, among other things. It's not essential for every possible topic to be covered. If the only book the library has about oceans looks dull, you can pass it up. There are plenty of other fascinating children's books. You could plan to read out loud to the kids at bedtimes in the hotel. You wouldn't have to have a plan to read certain books on certain evenings, but if you knew you were going to Sea World the next day, you might make a point of reading about dolphins beforehand.

On the day of your departure, you could load up the books, the kids' journals or notebooks and writing implements along with the luggage, and off you go. You may be thinking, "But what about math?" How you handle the 3 Rs while on vacation depends upon your situation. If your children are years above grade level in math, you may decide to have a math-free week. On the other hand, if your children are having difficulty with math, you may feel uneasy about letting them take the week off entirely. There are still more options. The children could do

Travel Time Tote

Creating a travel time tote is a great way for homeschoolers to ensure they have an easy way to bring school activities with them when they find themselves having to leave the house on the fly, thus enabling them to turn wasted time into learning time. A travel time tote is easy enough to create. Take a simple knapsack, book bag, or duffle bag, and fill it with any of the following, to be determined by the age of your child.

- Paperback book.
- Math worksheets such as Calculadder pages.
- Pens and pencils, as well as a pencil sharpener.
- Crayons or markers.
- A book about the states—great to read on the run.
- Notebook.
- Coloring books.
- Puzzle books, crosswords, and so on.
- Math and state capital wrap-ups.
- Copies of current vocabulary or spelling word lists, for practice.
- A science or history overview book.
- Clay or Play-Doh.
- Snacks that don't crush or mess easily.
- Yo-yos or small toys for younger children.
- Small puzzlelike toys, such as Rubik's cube or Word Spin.
- Story starter cards—you can make these yourself by taking a dozen index cards and writing simple sentences on them to elicit a story, such as: "If you could make one wish, what would you wish for?" Or "If you had the ability to fly, where would you go?"

math lessons on a few Saturdays before the trip to make up for the days that will be missed or could do extra lessons during some evenings as "homework." Instead of your usual math lessons, you might opt to bring along a game such as Math-it. Board games using dice give young children practice counting and adding up small numbers. You can have the child budget his souvenir money. However you handle math, or any other subject while vacationing, make sure it's all done in the spirit of fun.

You'll need to decide how to deal with language arts and any other subjects that are part of your usual school day. You could have the children do journal writing in the evening or write a letter to Grandma. The children could present a simple oral report to the family about something interesting they learned at Sea World or from talking to the guide at the museum. After a day on the beach, you might declare it to be silent reading time for the kids while Mom and Dad sit on the hotel balcony enjoying the salty breeze and sipping their cool beverages of choice. Keep in mind that this is just one way of homeschooling during a family vacation. Each homeschooling parent can decide which strategies will work best in his or her family. Some parents love spontaneity and can spot a teaching opportunity, snap it up, and delight their children while improvising a lesson. Other parents would be uncomfortable with this style of teaching and would prefer to have a more precise school plan in place. That can also work well. The parent might choose to have one or two hours of the usual schoolwork scheduled into each day and might want to assign kids particular books to read that fit well with the activities planned for each day.

Unschooling parents may feel that the vacation experience itself is so ripe with opportunities for learning that no adult interference is required. This parent would just act as a facilitator to help the child pursue his or her interests. Regardless of which methods you use, ask yourself these questions now and then. Are they learning what I feel they absolutely must learn during this time? Are they learning it in ways that kindle their interest in learning rather than snuffing it out? However you handle homeschooling during these times, don't lose sight of the primary purpose of vacationing, which is rest, recreation, and fun!

Avoiding Burnout

Especially for the new homeschooler, it is not uncommon to feel overwhelmed by all you have to do. When your self-doubts and worries cause you to focus all your energy on just making it through another homeschool day, and you've forgotten how to enjoy schooltime with your children, take a deep breath and relax. There is probably no need for your feelings of urgency because, most likely, you have a number of years left in which to ensure that your children learn everything they need to learn before graduation. So, take some time to give a little thought to how to improve the situation so that you can return to being a happily homeschooling family once again. Take comfort in the knowledge that even some of the best homeschooling families suffer from burnout now and then.

Joy Days

Is it a glorious sunny day, and you and your children are itching to get outside? Why not take a break? You can build a certain number of 'joy days' into your school calendar the way many schools do for snow days. Joy days are days when you can call off school just to have fun. They aren't doctors' appointments or Aunt Alice's visit, but just because it is a glorious day and you feel like kicking back and enjoying yourselves.

You'll have to devise your rules for the use of joy days. First, design your school schedule so that you can incorporate a certain amount of them into the school year without missing a state attendance minimum. Do you want 5? Or are 10 days more your speed? Maybe you want to design a year-round school schedule, but build in 40 joy days? Look at your family and your lifestyle, and determine which approach will work best for you.

Next, determine who can declare a joy day. Can any child declare a joy day? Do all the kids have to agree to have one? Do all kids and the teaching parent have to agree? Can they be used several days consecutively, or do they have to be spread out at specified intervals? Do it however works best for your family.

Another approach, if it is within your state's legal structure, would be to declare a joy day during the week, when you feel you truly need it, and make up the day on a rainy Saturday afternoon later on in the year. Laura creates little tokens for her kids, which either child can opt to trade in for a joy day, but she reserves the right to veto if there is a good reason to do so. Also, the joy day must be paid back later within a certain timeframe. Laura notes the tentative date on the calendar, and the missed school day must be made up by this date. One caveat here, though: Make sure you *do* make up the day at a later time, or you'll find yourself having a rough time toward the end of the school year when the weather is calling you out to play and you've too many days to make up to stay in compliance!

Break Your Routine

Make today an alternate learning experience instead of the regular school day. This could mean spending the day gardening and reading about plants, taking a field trip to the museum or zoo, or anything else you can come up with. Remember, there are innumerable settings and situations in which learning can occur, so stay flexible. Sometimes, getting away from your usual routine for a day may be just what you and the kids need.

Time For You

There is one particular pitfall many homeschooling parents stumble into—neglecting to take care of themselves.

When you have too few hours in the day to begin with, it can be difficult to relax. How can you sit down and enjoy the luxury of losing yourself in a novel, a bubble bath, or a cup of coffee while watching the sunset when you've got a sink full of dishes, a mountain of laundry, and a list of at least 50 other things you've been meaning to get around to still left undone?

Beware of this trap. Sometimes it is necessary—*especially* for the homeschooling parent—to force yourself to step away and take time just for you. This won't happen, though, no matter how much you intend to make it happen, unless you schedule this time for you and honor it as an important and valid commitment.

If you step away and relax, you will often find you are far more productive upon returning to your duties. You will feel more energized, more relaxed, and you will deal with stress better. Try any of the following:

- Exercise.
- Meditation or prayer.
- A catnap.
- Reading time—somewhere where you will be uninterrupted.
- A bubble bath—uninterrupted by children or telephones!
- Journal writing.
- Chatting with friends.
- Going out for a cup of coffee.
- Enjoying a grown-up movie.
- Trying a new hobby or activity.

Yes, we know you're thinking, "But how can I find the time for this?" We admit this isn't easy. That is why you are going to have to schedule it. Swap baby-sitting with a friend or arrange for your partner to give you a regular time-out period. It is hard to be a homeschooling parent—you can easily develop cabin fever, but it can be alleviated by any of the above or anything else you particularly enjoy. The key is not so much what you do, but taking the time to do it for you.

(continued on page 142)

(continued from page 141)

Take the time for the things that make you feel good. A quick and rejuvenating shower on a hot summer afternoon can work wonders. Dressing nicely even when you've nowhere to go can put you in a more "together" mindset, as can styling your hair or putting on lipstick. Yes, you're a homeschooling mom, but you're also a person! Sometimes you can forget that—don't let this happen to you.

You can also link certain things to anchors throughout your day—an anchor being anything you do each and every day, such as meal times. Maybe you will even decide that every day right after lunch you will meditate for 15 minutes or each evening after dinner you will take a walk. Linking these activities to anchors will help you remember to take the time to do them, so that they don't slip between the cracks. If you take time to nurture yourself, you'll find it far easier to nurture your family.

Camp Weeks

Have you had it with multiplication tables and spelling words and can't bear the thought of another day of them? Up until now you haven't minded these staples of homeschooling. Right now, however, you've all gotten into a rut or perhaps fallen victim to the winter doldrums, and you find your previously eager learners groaning when you tell them it's time for school. A "camp week" may be just what your family needs to chase away the blues and undergo some healthy attitude adjustment.

Instead of your usual school program, plan to spend an extended period of time (a week usually does nicely) learning something new and different, doing a creative project, studying something interesting, making something, building something, or learning a new skill. Choose an activity that kids and the homeschooling parent can enjoy together. You might do arts and crafts, write and produce a skit, hold a cooking class, study aviation or space travel, do a science project, write a book, or anything at all that appeals to your family. You might wrap up the week by having a discussion about what you all learned. This chance to focus intensely on a learning activity of their choosing will serve to remind kids that learning can be fun.

Computer Days

Now and then you might allow your children to dispense with the pencils and spend the day doing "computer school." This can be carefully tailored to reinforce skills your children are currently studying, or you might opt to let them use any educational software available to them. If you have more than one child per computer, each one could do computer work on a different day or else take turns throughout the day. Since keyboarding or mousing nonstop for long periods of time can cause problems with one's hands, it's a good idea to make sure the computing kid takes breaks throughout the day.

Recreation

When life gets to be a grind, breaking out of the routine and doing something fun can be just what's needed to refresh everyone's attitudes about life in general and toward one another. If your kids have begun referring to you as the math drill sergeant rather than as Mom or Dad, it's time to take a break. Find something to do together that you can all enjoy, and so you can start being Mom and Dad again. You can play card games, do jigsaw puzzles, play basketball in the backyard, go to the movies, go roller skating, or anything that will be fun for the whole family. Of course, the ages and interests of your kids will help determine which activities you choose. Sometimes Julie's family sits around the kitchen table together with several activities going on at once, rather than one involving the whole group. Mike might play chess with Madeleine, while Martin draws a super hero and Isabel and Ross each do puzzles. Then Martin might play chess with Mike, while Madeleine and Julie work on a 500 to 1000 piece puzzle. Just being at the table together tends to get them all talking to one another.

Not every activity will be suitable for all members of your family, but it is also nice for each child to occasionally have some one-on-one time with Mom or Dad. Julie and Madeleine, age eleven, head out once in a while to the salon together for manicures and pedicures. They welcome the opportunity to hold a conversation without the younger siblings vying for attention. Sitting side by side with their feet luxuriating in the swirling warm water seems to melt away tension and encourage confidences.

Madeleine might ask about something she overheard an older kid say, or confide that her best friend is getting interested in boys, or that she's worried about her acne, or any number of things that she's been waiting for an opportunity to discuss with her mom. Sometimes they share giggles and the conversations never grow more profound than their nail color choices, but they always go home with Julie feeling closer to her eldest daughter and confident that they are maintaining a solid relationship.

Don't Forget the Basics

While we want to see you take time to nurture yourself as suggested above, it won't do much good if you ignore the basics of life, such as proper nutrition, rest, and relaxation. Remember, homeschooling can be challenging, and you need to take good care of yourself if you want to be the best you can be for both you and your family. Pay attention, and make sure you do the following:

- **Get enough sleep.** This is probably about eight hours per night but varies among individuals. If you suffer from insomnia, try the conventional sort of advice, such as warm baths at bedtime, relaxing bedtime rituals, and the like. There are books and health care professionals to help you, but, however you take care of it, treat insomnia as the important health issue that it is.

- **Eat healthy, well-balanced meals** at least three times per day.

- **Make time to exercise.** A brisk walk can do wonders to clear your head. Take the kids with you if you'd like, or walk when your partner is able to stay with them.

- **Find ways to cut out unnecessary or unrewarding stressors from your life.** Watch for volunteering more time than you reasonably can give or cooking elaborate meals when you don't have time, when you don't enjoy it, and it isn't really required anyway. If a child's behavior is the cause for your stress, expend the energy necessary to properly discipline him—sometimes it is tempting to let poor behavior slide if you're too tired to address it, but in the long run you will pay for it. A little energy spent on discipline in these sorts of situations can decrease the stress of family life.

Are You Worried Homeschooling Is Just Not Working For You?

Are you concerned that your children are not doing well in one or more subject areas, and you feel ready to throw in the towel? Don't quit yet, but consider the following:

- **Try using a different textbook, method, or material.** It could be that you are using a math text that is too repetitive—or not repetitive enough—for your children. If there are too many practice examples, your children may grow bored and inattentive once they've mastered that topic. Or, if there aren't enough examples, your children might not be able to keep up with all the new concepts that are being introduced.

- **Are you expecting too much seat work from an extremely active young child** who would do better with hands-on learning activities?

- **Are you using the best approach for your children?** Some children just can't learn visually, while others need to have visual aides, for example.

- **If reading is the problem, have you tried both phonics-based and sight word programs?** What works for one child may not necessarily work for the next.

- **Try to pinpoint the nature of the problem.** Read homeschooling books and articles to learn about different methods for teaching the problem subject or subjects.

- **Explore resources on learning disabilities. They often contain useful suggestions that anyone can apply.** There are websites and books on how to teach children with learning disabilities, which often have great tips for teaching a child who is struggling with a particular subject, even if your child has not been diagnosed with a learning disorder.

- **Discuss your difficulties with experienced homeschooling parents.** See if they know of any effective strategies you haven't tried yet.

- **Talk to professionals who may have some advice.** Seek advice from your pediatrician, schoolteacher acquaintances, or any other appropriate professionals if you need their help in sorting out what's going on with your children.

(continued on page 146)

(continued from page 145)

- **Try new materials.** One of the beauties of homeschooling is its flexibility. If you buy a math curriculum only to discover that it's not suitable for your children for some reason or another, there's nothing to prevent you from setting it aside to try a different program.

- **Look at your approach.** Maybe you are using a method that makes you uncomfortable, and it's causing you distress. Is your highly structured curriculum taking all of the fun out of homeschooling because you want to use your creativity more? On the other hand, perhaps you are in a state of constant panic because the unstructured approach you're trying leaves you worried that you aren't covering all you should. In that case, an organized, highly structured curriculum that clearly dictates what you must do may offer you the greatest peace of mind.

- **Are you making homeschooling too complicated?** Are you trying to teach too many subjects separately to too many children? Maybe you could teach some subjects such as science, social studies, and art together. On the other hand, maybe you are trying your best to teach three children science at the same time, but the young child keeps getting distracted and the older ones are bored. Maybe multi-age teaching just isn't going to work for you right now, though as they grow older you can certainly reconsider it.

- **Ease up.** Are you pushing your kids too hard or too soon? Do your children burst into tears when you show them their math page? Does it take them an hour to write five sentences? Of course, they could be daydreamers, but consider the possibility that you might be asking the children to do work for which they just aren't developmentally ready. Not all children are ready to read in the beginning of the first grade.

- **Break work down more.** You might try dividing the work up into smaller portions, perhaps having the child do a third of his math three different times during the day. If he's still frustrated, try reviewing easier work for awhile and easing him into the harder stuff.

- **Try using games to teach concepts that are frustrating your children.** Oftentimes reframing a difficult idea in a fun way can be the key to reaching your children. If your children just don't seem to be ready for formal reading instruction, you might give it up and try it again in a month or so.

- **Take time each day to relax.** Plan a break for yourself sometime during the afternoon or evening, and, for 30 minutes or so, read a book or magazine that has nothing to do with homeschooling, take a bubble bath, listen to music, or do whatever will take away some of the day's stress.

If you can't possibly find time to do things for yourself such as exercise and reading, you probably are someone who could benefit greatly from these sorts of self-care routines.

CHAPTER 21

Raising Responsible Kids

Academic success alone is not enough to ensure a child's success in life. A well-educated person who is lazy, never pitches in for the good of the team, can't be counted on to do what he or she promises, and never does a task without first being told to do it, is unlikely to excel in his or her personal or professional life. Qualities such as industry, persistence, responsibility, and initiative are worth cultivating in your children, and homeschooling parents are in an excellent position for that. They can model the character traits they wish to instill in their children and insist that they behave in ways consistent with these ideals. Of course, all conscientious parents do this to a degree, but the homeschooling parent has the advantage of time. Since they spend the entire school day with their children, they have many opportunities throughout the day to nudge behaviors in desired directions.

Chores

Learning to work and work hard will serve your children well in adult life, and requiring them to do chores is a good way to begin the process. By age three or four, most children are ready to start doing simple chores. They can pick up their toys, put clothes in the hamper, put their folded laundry in a drawer, set the table, help carry groceries in from the car, and more. Older children can tackle more complex tasks, such as doing the dishes and vacuuming carpets.

How do you get them to do it? There are many different approaches suggested by parenting experts for getting kids to do their chores, but there are a few basic guidelines that, if followed faithfully, usually make the task easier. First, come up with a plan of who does what when. Your children may be more cooperative if you let them help with the planning and take their preferences into account. You can make each child responsible for certain duties, for example, taking out the trash or emptying the dishwasher, or you can come up with some sort of rotating schedule so that everyone takes turns with the various chores.

Once you have worked out who is going to do what and how often, you will need to make sure that each child knows precisely what is expected of her. While it is obvious to most adults that a bedroom isn't tidy when it has dirty dishes and candy wrappers sitting on the nightstand, the obvious may need to be spelled out for kids. It's often helpful to list very specific instructions for completing any chore that involves multiple steps and post them in a convenient place for the children to refer to as needed. Instructions for tidying a child's bedroom, to give an example, might include items such as "place dirty clothing in the hamper, empty the wastebasket if it is more than half full, pick up items off the floor that don't belong there, throw away trash, and bring dirty dishes to the kitchen sink." Some chores entail learning specific skills, so be prepared to help the child to load the dishwasher a few times, or to wash, dry, and fold a load of laundry. Once you're confident that the child is capable of doing the chore without your help, you can step out of the way.

When you assign a chore to a child, it should be clear that doing the chore is an absolute requirement rather than an option. One of the simplest ways to teach your child a healthy work ethic is to show him that you take work, yours and his, seriously. Resist the temptation to let

Teaching Your Teen Time Management

Some people seem to be born organized, while others have to work at it. If you need to help your teen manage her time better, here are a few simple suggestions that can help instill habits that will make adult life much easier:

- **Create a Plan.** Each week, have your teen make a master list of all the tasks she needs to do that week.

- **Use Routine to Reinforce the Basics.** Have him develop a morning routine that includes assigned chores, getting dressed for the day, and breakfast, all which are to be accomplished by schooltime. If the teen needs a memory aid, have him use a checklist to make sure tasks don't get forgotten.

- **Cut Out Distractions.** It's often helpful to require that the morning routine be accomplished prior to any television watching or electronic gaming, especially if your teen tends to become so absorbed in them that she forgets to do her chores and get ready for school.

- **Look at the Day Ahead.** Each morning the teen can take a moment to make a list of the things he plans to do that day. Specifically it can include school assignments (or not, depending on your homeschooling style), places to go to, such as dentist appointments and social outings, and items to obtain that day, such as library books or other resources.

- **Teach the Teen to Be Prepared.** Encourage the teen to spend a few moments at bedtime preparing for the next day. This could involve things like tidying up her desk so it's ready for her to use the next morning and looking over the next day's plans and locating any particular items she will need, including clothing.

- **Reap the Rewards.** Give your teen the option of earning a long weekend by getting the week's work done early. Let him reap the rewards of hard, focused work.

kids' chores slide because enforcement is such a nuisance. Have some sort of mechanism for making sure that chores get done as assigned. You might have a rule that chores must be done by a certain hour or they will face an unpleasant consequence, for example, no playing after school that day.

Julie's family uses a system that rewards the children for hustling and getting their jobs completed promptly. Her three older children are required to make their beds, tidy their bedrooms, get dressed, comb their hair, eat breakfast, and brush their teeth each morning. Martin unloads the dishwasher, while Madeleine feeds the cats. After all their morning chores are done, they are free to play until schooltime.

If they stay focused and work without dawdling too much, they usually can have 30 minutes to an hour of free time prior to school. If they aren't finished by schooltime, they lose their right to play with friends, watch television, or play computer games after school that day. The parents rarely have to impose these sanctions. Prior to implementing this simple system, the two older kids were regularly taking about two hours to do 30 minutes' worth of chores, and no amount of parental nagging seemed to improve the situation. Now they are easily getting them done with time to spare.

Laura's family uses chore charts, which are displayed so that they are highly visible. The charts serve as both reminders and motivators, for when her boys complete an assigned chore they place a sticker on their charts. When they achieve a certain amount of points (stickers), they receive a reward, in the form of a privilege.

Other parents make the child's allowance contingent upon completion of chores, though many believe that it's not a good idea to pay kids for chores so they can learn to work in the spirit of contributing to the family rather than simply because they can acquire material things.

Self-Motivation

When your children go off to college, you're not going to be around to remind them to brush their teeth and put their dirty clothes in the hamper. So at some point, they need to learn to carry out their responsibilities without being told, nagged, or reminded repeatedly. With this goal in mind, it's a good idea to find ways to have the children shoulder the responsibility for making sure chores get done when they are required.

You can have a child use an alarm clock to make him responsible for getting up on time each morning. You might want to resist the temptation to wake up a child who turns off the alarm and falls back asleep, because it deprives him of an opportunity to learn a lesson about responsibility. At first, you can help him remember to set the alarm at bedtime and then drop the reminders when the habit has become firmly ingrained.

Whatever system you use to ensure that chores get done, your family life will be more pleasant if you avoid wheedling, cajoling, or threatening your children when they don't seem to be making adequate progress through morning chores. If a young child seems genuinely to have been sidetracked, it might be appropriate to remind her that it's chore time and to please stop playing with toys when she is supposed to be picking them up.

On the other hand, if you find a 10-year-old reading comic books when he is supposed to be doing chores, you might decide not to intervene and let the child experience the consequences of not getting his or her work done. It helps if the consequence is something preestablished, so when you say "no TV for you today," the kid will have no one to blame but himself. The consequence could be the loss of a privilege, such as television watching, having friends over to play, or computer gaming, or it could be the addition of a not-very-pleasant chore after school that day.

Whether or not you adopt a system of rewards to help in teaching your kids to do chores, letting the children experience the natural consequences of failing to carry out their responsibilities whenever practical can teach powerful lessons. This means not rushing in to protect the children from uncomfortable results of their irresponsible behavior. If Susan doesn't do her laundry as she's required to and finds that when she gets ready to go to the movies with her girlfriends, she has nothing clean to wear, she will realize that she has to stay home and do laundry instead of going out for a nice afternoon at the theater. After a few occasions on which friends come to call but your child can't go out to play because he hasn't finished his chores yet, your child may get the message that there is a benefit in taking care of things as soon as possible, for example, it frees him up to take advantage of opportunities that unexpectedly come his way. Obviously, there are situations in which it's not appropriate to allow natural consequences to occur, such as when real injury might be the result or if you're confident that the child is already committed to not repeating the mistake. The goal isn't to be cruel, but just to avoid enabling irresponsible behaviors.

If a child has trouble remembering to do a particular chore or two, it's reasonable to help him or her come up with ways to remember as long as the responsibility is ultimately left with the child. An older kid might use the alarm on a wristwatch to remind him that it's nearly schooltime. If you use a chore chart, the child can be responsible for reviewing it to make sure items aren't forgotten. Encourage each child to check off items as completed and then report to you when the chores are all done. You can opt to do a quick inspection or forgo inspection entirely if the child has reliably been doing what he's supposed to do. However, you might want to check on occasion, just to ensure that standards are kept up.

Whether or not you use any sort of structured approach to homeschooling, building some routines into the child's day will help her develop the habit of doing things that need to be done. The routines can be as simple as doing morning chores upon waking, picking up clutter before dinner, or spending a few moments at bedtime rounding up items that will be needed the next morning. Whichever routines you decide to establish, making sure that they are followed consistently will help them become habit. After the habits are firmly ingrained, if you have to deviate from them now and then, it probably won't undo what they've learned, as long as you get back on track as soon as possible.

As children grow older, you can give them more and more chores. There is a lot of work involved in maintaining a household, and busy homeschooling parents really can't do it all. Older kids can be responsible for doing their own laundry from start to finish. They can sweep and mop the floors, vacuum carpets, wash windows and cars, prepare food, and more. Delegating a substantial portion of the work to your children will benefit the entire family.

Supervising Siblings

Older children can be taught to take partial responsibility for the care of younger siblings. An 8- or 10-year-old can entertain a toddler while a parent cooks dinner or mops the kitchen floor. He or she can read to the little one, serve him or her snacks and drinks, and lend assistance in a number of ways. As the child grows older and more experienced, the responsibilities can become more complex. You might assign a preteen

Self-Directed Learning

At this stage, a teen can take a major role in his educational planning. How much autonomy you allow him in the planning of his school program is something you will have to work out for yourself. Some teens already know where their lives are headed, and parents know that they can let the kids figure out the particulars. These parents are comfortable in functioning merely as friendly advisers. Parents of a teen whose pursuits of life goals aren't clearly focused might understandably want to retain more control. They might insist that the usual high school subjects be covered, then encourage the teen to choose some elective subjects. You might require her to spend some hours studying a topic she chooses or learning some new skill instead of her spending countless hours watching television.

Before the beginning of the school year, you can sit down with your teen and together come up with a tentative plan for the year. You might list books to be read, math chapters to be completed, papers to be written, and other learning activities along with target dates for their completion. The more you take the teen's preferences into account, the more likely he will be committed to his independent study plan. You can plan regular meetings to discuss progress, revise goals if needed, and occasionally change course if the need arises.

Keep in mind that a homeschooled teen often is able to learn most subject matter independently, with the help of textbooks or other resources and a little parental oversight. A homeschooled teen has the unique opportunity of being able to spend a large part of her day studying what interests her the most. You will probably find that your teen will have more discretionary time than her public school friends. There are a couple reasons for this. Not having to ride the school bus and travel a distance frees up an hour or more in most cases. Your teen can spend the early morning hours doing chores and satisfying the basic requirements of her educational program. The rest of the day can then be used to develop other talents and skills. If your teen has a passion for art, music, or computer programming, she can devote time to those pursuits.

to baby-sit the toddler or preschooler while you paint the bathroom or organize a closet. It's a good idea to convey to the older child the seriousness of the duty, for example, that he is responsible for keeping the little one safe and out of mischief. You can check on them frequently, and give pointers as needed until the older child proves that he can safely handle this responsibility. Letting the child know you're depending on him to fulfill this important responsibility can really help the child develop self-confidence and instill a sense of responsibility.

Household Projects

Mastering adult skills such as household chores and child care will help children learn to view themselves as competent human beings, and to take this a step further, you may want to include them in the occasional large project. Are you planning to remodel your kitchen or paint your home? If you get creative, you can probably think of ways to involve your entire family in the process and can give your kids the experience of functioning as the member of a team working toward a common goal. The key to a successful experience is to expect to work at a relaxed pace and find for each child useful work that is within his ability. Make sure each child can successfully perform whatever tasks you delegate to him. Little kids can fetch tools and paint a little (if you dare!) Young children will probably only stick to a task for a few minutes at a time, so plan for them to be able to entertain themselves nearby while you and the others are working. Older children can help choose paint colors and flooring and help with painting and wallpapering. A teen may be able to take a much more adultlike role in the process, depending upon his or her experience and maturity. The project may even afford the teen an opportunity to take a leadership role, such as directing the work of younger siblings.

Allow plenty of time for the project, because having to hurry will only frustrate all involved. In some cases, you could probably do it more quickly without your children's "help," but think of the time you spend painting with them now as an investment in the future—both theirs and yours. In a few years, they'll be of great help to you when doing such projects, and they'll have the skills and confidence to tackle them after they leave the nest.

Family Night

As a devoted parent you probably know the value of time spent together as a family. Sometimes this is hard to accomplish as a homeschool family, which may surprise you since you are together all the time when you homeschool. But it is easy to get caught up in learning and child rearing and forget to make time for pure recreation together. This can be solved in part by incorporating some of the suggestions we've given in this book to make learning more fun, but you will also find that sometimes you have to work at taking some time to just kick back and relax together.

If you're like most of us, you have really good intentions. You want to take time off with the kids, but it seems you never get around to it. There's always more laundry to do, lesson plans to be made, or errands to run. We know—we've been there. What we have discovered is that the only way to ensure time for recreation is to set it aside intentionally. Create an official "family night" and keep that time sacred.

Simply designate one night (or weekend afternoon) per week or even during alternate weeks if that's all you can sincerely manage, and log it on your calendar as "family night." Refuse to let anything other than extreme circumstances interfere with it. Then sit down with your children and come up with a list of activities you'd like to do together. It may take a bit of creativity to find things that everyone will enjoy. However, you can usually find a way to accomplish this.

You might even consider allowing your children to invite a guest to family night. This is one way to encourage a child to spend this time together, especially if they are yearning to be out with friends. Then again, you also have the option of insisting that this is family-only time. Whatever you do, make sure you are all together. In this day and age, that accomplishment alone is a feat!

If you are stumped for activities, consider some of the following:

- bowling
- roller skating
- miniature golf
- picnic in the park
- board games
- movies and popcorn

(continued on page 158)

(continued from page 157)

- seeing a movie together
- making your own sundaes (or cookies, candy, cakes)
- going to the park together
- reading aloud together

So, now that you've got some suggestions to get you started, come up with a system to decide who chooses what to do when, and begin!

The Rewards

Raising your children to be hard-working, competent, self-confident people takes effort, consistency, and self-discipline on your part. There will be times when you're tired or frustrated and would prefer to do things yourself rather than insist that the children do what they are supposed to do. Or you may feel guilty about asking your children to "do too much." Investing time now to teach your children skills they'll need later is a gift to your children that they will appreciate when they are adults living on their own or with their own families. Besides, long after they grow up and leave their childhood home, when they get together for holidays, your sons and daughters will laugh about the time they helped paint the kitchen.

CHAPTER 22

Making Work Count

As your children negotiate the teen years, working outside the home can add another dimension to increasing independence and responsibilities that help ease the transition into adult life. It can reinforce the work-related values and skills you have been teaching at home, such as responsibility, punctuality, and completing tasks. Most any job can fulfill this function, but carefully chosen work experiences can be valuable additions to a teen's education. The teen can gain experience in job hunting and interviewing, working with people from a variety of backgrounds, serving customers and dealing with the public, and whatever other skills the particular job requires. Earning money provides an opportunity to teach the teen a bit about fiscal responsibility, as well.

Volunteering

Nonpaying work offers its own set of rewards. It can let a teen experience the satisfaction of giving to others and can be a way to obtain specific job skills. Perhaps your teen has hopes of becoming an elementary schoolteacher or a pediatrician. Doing volunteer work involving children can give your son a feel for what it is like to work with little kids, especially if he has no young siblings. He might volunteer to assist with coaching a community child's soccer team, assist with the children's choir or church school class, or participate in a program for disadvantaged kids.

There are so many needs for volunteers that there is bound to be some activity that will be personally satisfying to your teen, while teaching him useful skills. One teen we know volunteered her time in the church office, gained secretarial experience, and learned how an office works, while helping out her church at the same time. Another did computer training for some senior citizen volunteers for a charitable organization. There are many different ways in which your child can use her skills to help others, while gaining valuable work experience in the process.

Steps Toward a Career

A part-time job can be a way for high school students to test out possible career paths they are considering. Homeschooled teens have a wonderful opportunity to work in the field of their interest, in some aspect, either through volunteering or through part-time jobs. Since they are not in conventional schools, they can be available during hours that other teens are in school. If you use your teens' jobs as part of your curricula, your teens can probably meet your state's legal requirements while obtaining solid real-world skills.

The teen who thinks he might want to become a veterinarian could get a clearer understanding of what a veterinarian's workday is like by working for a veterinary practice. This experience might help solidify the kid's plans to attend veterinary school, or it might prevent him from spending a year or two on tuition only to discover he dislikes dealing with sick animals.

If your teen aspires to become a business owner, she might find a position in a small business where she can see first hand the work that goes into running a business of one's own. Also, a small business will often afford the teen opportunities to participate in many different aspects of the business. Most teens who work are motivated primarily by their desire to earn money, so when one comes along with an enthusiasm to learn the business inside and out, it's bound to impress an employer. As the kid proves her worth, the business owner is liable to give the teen increasing levels of responsibility. This sort of work experience can prove invaluable.

Apprenticeships

Are your children interested in a trade or skill that can be learned on the job? Perhaps there is someone who would be willing to teach them. Scrutinize your mental list of friends, relatives, neighbors, church members, fellow soccer parents, business associates, and other acquaintances for suitable mentors for your teens. People who have never worked with an apprentice and have never considered such an arrangement can sometimes be persuaded with the right approach. We know a young man who pursued this option and today works in graphic design for a newspaper. When he was 16, he went to the owner of a print shop, earnestly expressed his desire to learn the business, and offered to work for free in order to learn whatever he could. The kid was smart, enthusiastic, and eager to do a good job. The owner soon learned his worth, and subsequently paid him well. By the time he went to college, he'd accumulated substantial experience in his chosen field. This young man is just one example of how successful this approach can be. Many teenagers have found this to be a logical path to their career.

A Job's a Job

There is, of course, the possibility that your teens won't find employment in fields they would like to some day pursue full time. This could be for many different reasons—perhaps the economy is shaky when your teens are job hunting, perhaps they're interested in fields that don't make this a practical option (though we have found that usually there is some way to have your children work around people who do the jobs that the children eventually aspire to do, even if it is merely clerical work), or perhaps the industry just doesn't exist in your geographical location.

Does this mean that any work experience your children gain at this time will be wasted? Absolutely not! Your teens can work anywhere—even in the local burger joint and still learn a tremendous amount of skills.

They can learn how to interact with coworkers, how to handle uncomfortable situations such as asking for a raise or a change in schedule to accommodate a special event in their lives, and how to interact with customers. There are also the important nuances of business they can pick up. The teen who dreams of someday owning her own business may, as described above, carefully watch her boss, a small business owner, to learn about managing her own business. There is no reason a teen working even in a fast food restaurant or local supermarket can't learn from these experiences as well—many of the experiences she learns in such a setting can be applied in other areas in ways she won't even be able to foresee at the time. Very little experience in the workforce, as in life, is wasted.

So, if your children can't find work related to the fields they dream of, encourage them to get jobs nonetheless so that they can gain practical world experience. They will be even better employees (or business owners, or doctors) in the future because of it, and they will likely have a greater appreciation for the work they eventually do because of their experience working in a field that is less than their ideal (again, important training for life, in general).

If you agree with all this, but feel your children still need to gain a clearer understanding of the fields they wish to pursue, try setting aside schooltime each day for them to research those fields. Have them read biographies on people who have worked in their fields and trade magazines they would be required to study if they worked in those fields already. You may also want to encourage them to visit Internet bulletin boards and Web pages where people in those professions tend to discuss current topics, so that they gain an even clearer understanding of the fields. While this may not serve as a substitute for an apprenticeship or position in the area of their interest, it will at least ensure that they are cultivating a growing understanding of what working in those industries will be like. Couple that with work experience in general, and your teens will receive good foundations for understanding the work world. Remember, a job *is* a job, and in the real world we don't always have the option to choose our ideal position and may have to approach employment in just this way—working at the less than ideal while gaining an education that will help move us closer to our goals. You can't get a more "real life" education than that.

Getting Hired

When you go for a job interview, there are some important things you should keep in mind if you want to put yourself in the best possible light.

- **Check Your Appearance.** While you may feel strongly about expressing your individuality, remember that the first thing a potential employer can see about you is what you look like. So take care in how you dress—be neat, clean, and well groomed. Tame down any clothing styles that reflect a wilder side that is uncommon if you want the interviewer to look beyond your clothing to who you are.

- **Make Eye Contact.** This is a very important factor that many people overlook. Eye contact establishes better communication and demonstrates active listening. It makes the other party feel you are paying attention and that you care about what they are saying. It also helps the other party see you as more honest. People who don't maintain eye contact are sometimes referred to as "shifty eyed," and people don't trust them. Even if you avoid eye contact because you are nervous, you may be sending a negative message that isn't even true!

- **Give a Firm Handshake.** A firm handshake demonstrates that you are confident.

- **Answer Questions Directly and Honestly.** If you feel uncomfortable when asked if you can do something you don't know how to do, admit you don't have this skill, but are dedicated to learning it as quickly and expertly as possible. Let the potential employer know you will be committed to doing whatever is necessary to fulfill your job obligations.

- **Be Polite!** Little things such as proper greetings, pleases, and thank yous go a *long way* in impressing employers since they want to know that you will be polite to customers or fellow employees. Of course, you must maintain this when interacting with people once you're hired, as well.

- **Don't Exaggerate Your Experience, but Present Yourself Fairly.** It isn't a good idea to say you have experience that you do not, for once you begin working, this will likely become evident. However, make sure you are giving yourself credit for all the things you *do*

(continued on page 164)

(continued from page 163)

know how to do. Many times there are skills we gain in volunteer jobs, special projects, or from participating in clubs, community activities, or church groups. They contribute to our being a potentially good employee, so make sure you tell the potential employer that you have assisted in the church office by typing letters or have acted as treasurer of your scout groups. The former would demonstrate some office experience for an office position, whereas the treasury experience would possibly help further sway an interview positively for someone applying for a position as a cashier.

- **Don't Fidget.** When you are being interviewed, don't fidget or look around distractedly. Keep focused and your interview will go better.

- **Try Not to Be Nervous!** Remember that everyone who is employed has gone through interviews, so whoever is interviewing you has been through this process before themselves. You will learn that this process gets easier as you go along and that interviewers are people just like you!

Money in the Real World

Now that your children are working, you have a new tool to help them learn the realities of money. If you've been following the suggestions in our math chapter, your children already have been learning some real-world math skills, such as budgeting with or without the aid of a computer program like Money or Quicken. Now, they can put this knowledge to practical use.

Give some thought to what lessons you want your teens to learn about money, and figure out any rules you'll need to implement regarding how they use their earnings. Oftentimes, when teens earn money they spend a great deal of it on pizza, movies, music CDs, stylish clothes, airbrushed fingernails, and other nonessentials. If you can't afford to spend $50 on your fingernails, you may feel it isn't appropriate for your teenaged daughter to have that luxury. On the other hand, maybe she is such a responsible, hard-working kid that you're glad for her to have that one indulgence. You might want your teens to pay for gasoline, clothing, or other practical items, or you might believe parents should foot the bill for these things. You'll probably want your teens to develop the habit of saving a portion of their earnings for college or other future needs, but how large a portion? These are the sorts of issues you'll need to consider so that you can formulate policies that are in line with the values you are striving to instill.

What about College?

What about college? This is another frequently asked question about homeschooling. Some parents fret over this from day one, while others feel they have plenty of time to worry about this issue. While college may seem far off in the future, it's not a bad idea to start thinking about it early in your children's homeschooling careers. With a little bit of advance planning, you can simplify the application process and help your homeschooled teens gain admission to their college or university of choice.

There is a good chance that you will have been keeping records of some sort all along, though some state laws require none and others simply require attendance records. If you keep a portfolio throughout the high school years, whether or not your child ever submits it with a college application, it will still be useful. A portfolio can help jog your teens' memory about what activities, awards, honors, and projects they ought to mention on college applications. Throughout the high school years, keep writing samples, a list of books read, examples of completed hobby or craft projects, photos, newspaper articles, or any other mementos chronicling your teens' activities so that when college application time rolls around, your teens will be presented in the best possible light.

Just before your homeschooled children reach their freshman year of high school is a good time to start gathering some preliminary information about colleges. In these early teen years, many students don't have much of an idea of which college they might want to attend, but you can probably make some educated guesses. You may want to choose a few schools from each these categories:

- Those in close proximity to your home.

- Those in a place your child dreams of living in during college, for example, New York City, the Rocky Mountains, or the West Coast.

- Those that offer outstanding programs in an area of study in which your child already displays particular talent or interest.

- Large schools with vast arrays of course offerings.

- Small schools with more personal learning environments.

- Any school that your child has a particular reason for considering among her options.

- If religious development is a goal in your family, schools that will support it appropriately.

After you choose some colleges, find out what their college admission requirements are and how a homeschooler can satisfy them. Even though it's still early in the process, by being aware of the requirements you can make sure they are being satisfied as you go along. A survey of 513 public and private universities conducted during the 1998–1999 school year found that only two of them had no policy established for evaluating homeschooled applicants. The numbers of homeschooled high school students have reached a level that most colleges and universities nowadays are becoming somewhat accustomed to working with homeschooled applicants. Some of these schools, however, have policies that many view as being unfairly discriminatory toward homeschoolers. They may require the homeschooled student to pass the General Education Development (GED) test, which offends many homeschooled teens and parents who feel that a good student shouldn't be required to take a test that has traditionally been used by high school dropouts. Some college admission offices require homeschooled applicants to undergo testing, such as the SAT subject tests (SAT-II), in addition to that which is required of traditionally schooled applicants. Homeschooling families with strong feelings on this discrimination issue decide to exclude from consideration those colleges and universities whose admission practices they deem unfair. On the other hand, other homeschoolers feel that it's perfectly reasonable for a college to require extra testing for homeschooled applicants, since evaluating these student based on grades issued by parents seems hardly fair to other applicants.

Choosing a College

You can consult reference books such as Barron's *Profiles of American Colleges*, magazine articles such as "America's Best Colleges" issue of *U.S. News and World Report*, and websites to find information about colleges and universities. Keep in mind that your goal is to help your teens gain admission to schools that are good fits; that is, the colleges and the teens need to suit each other, so you should consider much more than ratings of overall quality. A college may rank very high, but have a definite weakness in a particular program. On the other hand, some mediocre schools may excel in one particular program. If your teens already have definite plans to pursue particular careers, you will want to find out which schools offer programs that will best further their goals.

In addition to factors such as quality and types of degree programs offered, reputation, cost, and availability of financial aid, you should carefully consider the individual characteristics of your teens. Consider whether your teens will benefit more from the small class sizes and individual attention found in many small colleges or from the large selection of specialized course offerings found at many large universities. Their personality, preferences, strengths, and weaknesses will have an impact on how well they do at a given institution. It's worth considering whether the physical and social environments at a particular school are ones they can live in with a reasonable degree of contentment. It would be unfortunate to make the financial sacrifice necessary to send your bright homeschool graduate to an expensive private school, only to have him drop out because living in a noisy, crowded city is making him miserable. If there are any aspects of the demographics of the student body such as gender, race, or religious affiliations that are of special concern to your teens, be sure to consider these. Some young adults are so self-confident and adaptable that they don't mind being the only minority student in a classroom, whereas others might be very unhappy in that sort of situation. All of these issues are things for you to discuss with your college-bound teens.

Testing

Most colleges and universities require applicants to submit scores from either the ACT assessment or the SAT I. Many institutions will accept scores from either test, whereas some specify one or the other. According to ACT, Inc., the not-for-profit organization that provides the test, the ACT test, which includes English, math, and science, is based on high school curricula, so students are usually more comfortable with it than they might be with tests having narrower content. The SAT I, according to the College Board, is designed to measure mathematical and verbal reasoning abilities. Most students take these tests in their junior or senior years of high school, and many take the test more than once in hopes that their scores will improve with experience, which they often do.

Many students do some sort of preparation for taking these tests, which may involve independently working through a test-prep book found in bookstores and libraries, using a CD-Rom or online test preparation program, or taking a formal test-prep classroom course. Homeschooled teens usually have considerably less test-taking experience than their conventionally schooled peers, so for them, test preparation may be of particular importance. Opinions are divided as to how effective these various sorts of test preparation are, but there are a couple of points to ponder. Teens who read a great deal and from a variety of sources have an advantage on the verbal portions of the SAT I. Test preparation courses which spread the program out over a relatively long period of time and incorporate practice in using information learned are probably more effective than crash courses packed with rote memorization of vocabulary word lists and the like. Learning unfamiliar words, using them in sentences, and incorporating them into the teens' permanent vocabulary are more likely to improve test scores than temporarily memorizing them. Regardless of what form the teens' test preparation programs take, it's essential that they be aware of appropriate test-taking strategies, such as pacing and saving time-consuming questions for last. They need to learn the guidelines for guessing when they aren't sure of the correct answer. On the SAT, for instance, it's best not to guess if one has no clue as to the correct answer, but educated guesses may be worthwhile. They can read test-prep books for whichever test they are planning to take or read information from the College Board or ACT organization online to find this sort of information.

Prior to taking the SAT I, many students take the PSAT/NMSQT (Preliminary SAT/National Merit Scholarship Qualifying Test). They usually do this in their junior year. It's a good practice run for taking the SAT I and is also used to identify candidates for the National Merit Scholarship program. Homeschooled teens can take this test by contacting a public or private school and arranging to take it there. The SAT II tests are designed to demonstrate a high school student's degree of mastery of individual subjects such as English, math, science, history, social studies, and foreign languages. Some colleges include several of them in their admissions requirements, or homeschooled teens may decide to take them anyway in order to prove that they are highly qualified for admission to the colleges of their choice.

Other tests some homeschooled college-bound teens opt to take are the AP (Advanced Placement) and CLEP tests to earn credit for college-level work they have done without having taken a college course in one or more subjects. These exams are both produced by the College Board, the same organization responsible for the SAT. By scoring well enough on a number of these subject-specific tests, some teens are able to shorten their time spent in college by a year or more. Different colleges have different policies regarding their awarding of credit for either or both of these exams, so find out the particulars for colleges your teens are considering.

What Do Colleges Look for in Applicants?

Along with transcripts or portfolios, and test scores, your teens may have to include an essay in their application packets. A well-written essay can really contribute to a positive impression of your teen, so have him take plenty of time to do a good job with it. Homeschooling websites with information for college-bound teens often have sample application essays your teens can peruse to get an idea of how they are done.

In addition to high levels of academic achievement, colleges look for certain personal qualities in an applicant. When most of us were in high school, we were encouraged to participate in a variety of extracurricular activities and community services that would give college admissions personnel an impression of us as being well rounded. So, many of us dutifully played on sports teams, ran for student government offices or served on committees, volunteered at a local homeless shelter, played in the marching band, attended chess club or Spanish club meetings after school, and the like.

While these can be worthwhile endeavors, many of us weren't attending Spanish club due to our passion for the language and culture, but rather to enhance our appearance of being well rounded. This phenomenon didn't go unnoticed by college admission's offices, so now the quality we call "well rounded" is not the primary factor sought by many of the more competitive schools today. Instead, they are looking for an indication of a strong commitment to a single focus. The teen computer whiz who forms her own company and designs and markets her own game may be a more likely candidate for acceptance at her college of choice than the football player who plays in the school's marching band and participates in the computer club, without showing great depth of commitment to any one of these endeavors. So, you shouldn't worry too much if your teen is the youngest citizen ever to serve on the city council but doesn't have time for a variety of extracurricular activities, or if your young writer spent most of his free time writing a novel that has been accepted for publication, leaving little time for joining organizations and playing sports. When your teen does work with others on a project in which she displays admirable adult qualities such as leadership, desire for service to others, responsibility, or the like, she can ask an adult familiar with her work to write a personal recommendation to include in her college admissions packets.

About Transcripts and Portfolios

When the time comes for your high school student to begin filling out college applications, most likely you will be creating a transcript as well. This need not be cause for alarm, and you can let go of your concerns that your child's transcript will stand out like a sore thumb among the "official" transcripts of the other applicants. The fact is, college admissions offices are accustomed to receiving a vast assortment of transcripts from many different high schools, and you can produce a very official-looking document using a computer and any word processing program. You might look at a few transcripts to get ideas for creating one for your homeschooled student. As you peruse homeschooling Web pages that provide information for families with college-bound homeschooling teens, you will find samples of transcripts, or you might study ones that homeschooling families you know have used successfully.

There are a few basic elements that all transcripts include; namely the student's name, Social Security number, name and address of the high school, the names of the courses the student has completed, and the date the transcript is issued. Then there are a number of other items that not every high school includes in its transcripts, such as credits, grades, and grade point average. Homeschoolers who follow a traditional school-at-home approach will have been receiving grades all along, so they can simply be recorded on the transcript. Other homeschoolers are philosophically opposed to grades and have never used them. This really is not much of a problem when applying to colleges. It is no secret to college admissions personnel that grades assigned to a student by his or her parent are not entirely unbiased, so they tend to place more stock in other predictors of college performance, such as course descriptions, SAT scores, essays written by the student, and personal recommendations. Some homeschooling parents simply use a pass/fail grading system, while others leave off grades completely. If your transcript includes grades, also include a brief explanation of your grading system. "93–100% equals an A," or "A = average," or "A indicates mastery." A small college is less likely to insist on information like credits and GPA whereas a large university with thousands of applicants to evaluate may prefer that the homeschool transcript contain letter grades, GPA, credits earned, and even class rank! If you must, you can assign your high school student grades after the fact, and different homeschooling parents choose different ways of handling this. Some parents give their children an A in every subject because their homeschooling program always involves having a child continue with each subject until he or she mastered it. Others think it is best to only award an A grade in the subjects that the homeschooled teen has put in his or her best effort and excelled. There are many other ways parents devise to come up with grades when they are required to do so for consideration for financial aid or admission to a college.

Like grades, credits for course work completed are transcript items that are often not natural elements of a homeschooling high school program. Many times the homeschooled teen's studies, projects, and activities don't fit tidily into traditional categories, so the parent will have to make decisions such as, "does that play she wrote and produced count as English class or drama?" Since many interests pursued by homeschooled students are interdisciplinary, spanning several fields of knowledge, it can be a bit inconvenient to wrestle them into traditional subject categories, but it can be done. Some parents actually count hours spent doing various learning activities and use a standard formula to calculate credit, but that involves a good deal of record keeping. Others use a more relaxed method and award credit for a subject when the teen has done enough work to fulfill the requirements of a similar course in a public or private school. If all this seems a little artificial, well, it is. But giving college admissions offices the type of information they require will help make the whole process go smoothly. Yes, it will seem silly when you rank your homeschooled teen as one in a class of one, but so be it.

While most homeschooled college applicants submit transcripts and most colleges require or prefer them, some homeschoolers submit a portfolio rather than a transcript. A portfolio contains samples of the student's writing and other work, awards, or other evidence of their achievement, and this generally takes much longer to evaluate than a typical transcript. Some universities require a portfolio of a student's work for admission to a particular program, such as art, and small colleges are more likely to be willing to accept a portfolio in lieu of a transcript. If a teen has done something particularly impressive, showing the results of his or her work can make a positive impression. This might be a magazine article the teen had published, business cards, photos, and comments from satisfied customers documenting the teen's entrepreneurial endeavors, photos, and a written description of an award-winning science project or any other items that help demonstrate what a mature, committed, responsible, talented, innovator or go-getter the teen is.

Some Final Words

You and your family can get through the college admission's process just as you got through any number of homeschooling crises over the years. When your homeschooled child leaves the parental nest, whether to head off to an institute of higher learning or to follow some other life path, you can be satisfied that you have given him something of great value, an education supported by caring, committed parents.

A Few Extra Pointers

Our 10 Favorite Teaching Tools

Microscopes and Telescopes

Arguably these could be two tools, but we decided to put them together as they are both "scopes." These are among our most favorite tools in our homeschool. The universe is a vast and exciting place, and microscopes and telescopes open up a view of worlds of wonder for your children that they may never even have dreamed of.

A good microscope reveals hidden minuscule worlds teeming with life, while a good telescope enables your children to take a closer look at objects located light years away. Invest in good equipment, though, when it comes to these particular items, since you tend to get what you pay for. Some science supply companies sell used or refurbished microscopes at good discounts, so be sure to shop around.

Maps and Globes

Maps and globes can really help children better understand the world, its peoples, history, and current events. Try keeping a globe or a world map in a visible, easily accessible place. Then your children can refer to it frequently. Train your children to locate the places they are learning about. This will help them put things into context. For instance, before reading a book such as *Little House on the Prairie*, you can point out where the first colonies in the United States were located and trace the trail to the West where families settled as the United States became more populated. Explain that it is in this western area that families like the Ingalls had started new lives. This is just one of the many, many situations in which you can use a map or globe to help your children have a clearer understanding of what you are talking about.

Timelines

We love to use timelines, because as with maps, they help your children put people, places, and events into proper perspective. It is easy to get confused as to when a territory was settled, or when Mozart lived, but if you chart it on a timeline, your children will begin to understand the chronology of world history. Better yet, they may begin to recognize patterns. They will see the schools of thought and different movements across time, such as the Renaissance, or the Enlightenment. This will help them solidify their understanding of how the world was structured and which things perhaps influenced others in a way they otherwise might not see.

VCRs, DVD Players, and Cable TV

There are some homeschoolers who would be shocked to see these electronic items listed as homeschool tools, as a fair number of homeschoolers dislike television and go so far as to ban it from their home. While we understand their sentiments, we find that intentional use of cable television and a videocassette recorder (or DVD player) adds to homeschooling life. Time Warner cable is our cable provider and they have a "Cable in the Classroom" program (www.cic.com) where you can find listings of educational programs as well as support materials such as worksheets, Web-links that are related to the topic of interest, and even ratings and descriptions of programming. They also have a convenient mail alert service that e-mails notification of an upcoming program in your interest area.

As for using your VCR, look at educational films in your video store. Some of our local Blockbuster video stores have a "community service" area that loans you educational videos at no charge on a wide variety of topics. You can also look through your library's video selection to find materials to round out your curricula.

Cassette or CD Player

A cassette or CD player can enhance your homeschool in many ways. You can listen to foreign language instructional tapes or listen to a wide variety of music from around the world. This is even easier if your local library has audio items. However, music and foreign language aren't the only things you can use your music player for. You can also listen to audio books or record your tiny tykes talking away.

An older child can use a cassette recorder to play "reporter," interviewing family members for a genealogy report or to put together a collection of memories shared with him by family elders. This makes a terrific souvenir at family reunions, too!

Cuisenaire Rods

Cuisenaire rods are a measurement tool based on a cm square. They come in bright, attractive colors that help you distinguish one measurement from another. The basic cm square is beige, while the 2 cm one is red, for instance. This tool is very useful in teaching your child math concepts. It serves to clarify what you are teaching—for instance, 1 cm cube + 1 cm cube = a 2 cm one.

Cuisenaire also makes workbooks to go along with the rods that take your child through all kinds of learning experiences based on the rods. You will also find that some math curricula, such as Miquon Math, call for using Cuisenaire rods to solve some of the problems in their workbooks.

If you are looking for an easy-to-use premade manipulative for teaching math, Cuisenaire rods are the way to go.

Pattern Blocks and Tangrams

Pattern blocks are brightly colored blocks in the shapes of triangles, parallelograms, trapezoids, squares, and so forth. You use them to create nifty patterns, all the while demonstrating that you can combine them to create different geometric shapes. For instance, two triangles can create a square.

There are neat workbooks to support pattern blocks, in which you have to figure out which shapes to use to build the design. This is great for developing visual literacy, while being a nice change from Legos.

Tangrams are very similar, however they are typically sold as "logic puzzles" though they basically do the same thing. The Tangrams we have seen are plastic and smaller than the pattern blocks; however, they're just as much fun to use! Tangrams has a competitive aspect, in that you can race your partner to see who completes the picture first—although there's no reason you can't do this with pattern blocks as well.

The Arts and Crafts Box

While we mentioned the arts and crafts box in our art section, it bears mentioning again, as it truly *is* one of our very favorite tools for teaching. Having a box convenient and ready to use (not to mention one which makes clean-up simple!) is naturally encouraging when it comes to bringing out the artists in your children. Fill the box with whatever products you prefer, and encourage your children to use it whenever possible. Laura finds that her boys turn to it during free time, as naturally as they would to Legos or action figures. They see it as fun and as something that is a privilege. Laura sees it as a key to reinforcing the topics they have learned. When her boys were younger, she would have them simply draw a picture of what they learned today. Nowadays, however, she has them make full-blown presentations. Create as simple or elaborate a craft box as you believe your children will use, and see where things go from there!

Computer

We made it pretty clear in our computer chapter that a computer is perhaps our very favorite tool for teaching. With its wide variety of applications, from educational software to creative potential, it is easy to understand why. Install a modem and connect to the Internet, and you increase the benefits even further. If you don't have a computer, you may want to explore whether getting one is a viable option for you. At the very least, try checking out places that provide free access—many libraries have computers for public use.

Humor

It can be argued that humor isn't a tool, but we believe it is. We have found that every subject we explore becomes more interesting when we approach it playfully. This may be as simple as pausing when you read out loud—"Brandon, please demonstrate for us just what they mean when they said "Jake stomped through the woods like a famished beast desperately in search of his next meal." You'll all love the gales of laughter that follow such a demonstration. Try doing that with complicated science material, and you'll discover that your children recall the subject matter better—humor can be a great aid in helping them remember things that would otherwise be tedious to learn.

We try to inject a bit of humor into all our lessons. Feel free to be playful. Yes, your children need to study, and to learn, but do your best to have fun while doing it—you'll all appreciate this tool.

Games and Methods to Coax a Reluctant Learner

Sometimes it seems that no matter what you try, your child just doesn't seem interested in learning. This could be due to many different reasons, from insecurity, to boredom, to learning disabilities. If you think the problem is simply that you haven't captured your child's interest, try one of the following:

Unit Studies

Unit studies, especially "Units Out of the Blue" that you create based upon something that has captured your child's interest are sometimes the best way to grab your reluctant learner. Maybe Jen doesn't want to study science, but a new dinosaur film catches her eye. Take advantage of her interest to slide into a unit study—she won't realize she's "doing school" at first—at least not until she's already well under way, and by then she'll be having fun anyway and probably won't be bored at all. This is the perfect springboard into other topics.

Bingo

You can create your own BINGO game around virtually any subject. Use construction paper, poster board—whatever you want—to make up the game board, writing the subject areas on it clearly (with younger children you may be better off drawing pictures). From there, have your child use coins, chocolate chips, or any other small objects to mark off the objects as you call them. Many children love this game, and we know many homeschool parents who use this tool frequently.

Giant Step or "Mother May I?"

These two traditional childhood games can be incorporated into almost any school subject area to disguise learning as play. Simply have your children answer a question, solve a problem, or spell a word before they can take a giant step forward. Or, they can ask, "Mother May I take two steps ahead?" and you respond, "Yes, if you can spell Mississippi for me." Another variation of this can be played on a staircase, where your child can take one step up for each question answered correctly. Laura adds a component to her version in which the boys have to do something to make her laugh when they are close enough to almost win. This leaves them all in a fit of giggles and adds to the motivation to play another day.

"What Is It Like?"

To encourage a child who struggles with grammar, turn grammar into a game. When you are studying adjectives, for instance, ask your child to describe what something is like. Is that the Sun? Or is it the bright Sun? Or is it the bright, yellow Sun? Or the bright round sun? Or the hot, yellow Sun? See how many combinations your child can come up with. Again, you will find that humor goes a long way in playing these games.

Same or Different?

This is another game to play if your child is reluctant in a particular subject area. Ask your child to describe something exactly the same as whatever you are discussing . . . or completely different. This will help you gauge how much your child has comprehended, but it will also help your child learn to compare and contrast—and therefore to better grasp the subject being studied. For instance, if you described something the same as a frog, what would it be? Well, it hops. What else? Your child could describe a rabbit or kangaroo, but then realize that while these things hop or jump, they have very little in common with frogs. So ask what animals *do* have things in common. As you can see, this could be highly amusing, but also could teach your child a lot of information in the process.

Trade Off

If you don't seem to be reaching your children no matter what you do, try having your partner take over the subject area you are struggling with. Or perhaps get together with another homeschooling family to learn certain subjects together. For instance, maybe you will do science at Sally's house and art at your house. Sometimes just the change of atmosphere can make a difference, as can the companionship, particularly when going through a subject your children find particularly distasteful.

Hand Your Children the Reins

This may sound crazy at first, but if you ask your children how they would like to approach learning a particular subject, you may find that they have some good ideas. Perhaps they know what it is they want to learn or how they want to learn it. If not, sometimes just the empowerment your children feel when allowed to participate actively in determining what they are going to be learning and how they will be learning it can go a long way in breaking through a roadblock that formerly seemed insurmountable.

Shake Things Up

Do things that are different and unexpected. Start your day off serving dessert for breakfast (slip a scoop of ice cream onto waffles, or use whipped cream to make a face on your children's pancakes, for instance) or by announcing that today is backwards day. What does this have to do with helping a reluctant learner? Sometimes just the overall zaniness is enough to push a child past a barrier. Just make sure you carry the zaniness into the subject area your children are struggling with. If you are doing backwards day (where you walk backwards or everything perhaps means the opposite of what you say), tell your child who is struggling with math that he has to do his worksheet from the bottom up or to cross out all the subtraction signs and add the problems instead (as long as this is not more complicated than what he was doing to begin with!). Or perhaps give a reward for being the last to finish, giving a boost to the child who is frustrated at how slow he is in math. You know your child—you'll know if this would hurt her or make her giggle—use good judgment. The idea is to break the tension and make the day fun— this can go a long way in encouraging a child who is struggling.

State Homeschooling Laws

Alabama

Establish and/or enroll in a church school and file a notice with the local superintendent.

Teacher qualifications: None

Are particular subjects required? No

Record keeping: Maintain a daily attendance record to be kept by the church school

Testing: None

or:

Use a private tutor and file a statement with the local superintendent that shows children to be instructed, the subjects taught, and the period of instruction.

Teacher qualifications: Teacher certification

Are particular subjects required? Yes

Record keeping: Maintain a register of the child's work showing daily attendance and make such reports as the state board of education may require.

Testing: None

Arizona

Establish and operate a homeschool and file an affidavit of intent with the local superintendent.

Teacher qualifications: None

Are particular subjects required? Yes
Record keeping: None
Testing: None

Arkansas

Establish and operate a homeschool and file a notice of intent with the
   local superintendent.
Teacher qualifications: None
Subjects required: None
Record keeping: None
Testing: Yes

California

Qualify as a private school and file an affidavit with the local super-
   intendent.
Teacher qualifications: Must be "capable of teaching"
Subjects required: None
Record keeping: Maintain an attendance register
Testing: None

or:

Use a private tutor.
Teacher qualifications: Teacher certification
Subjects required: Yes
Record keeping: None
Testing: None

or:

Enroll in an independent study program through the public school.
Teacher qualifications: None
Subjects required: Yes
Record keeping: Yes
Testing: Yes

or:

Enroll in an independent study program through a private school.

Teacher qualifications: Must be "capable of teaching"

Subjects required: Yes

Record keeping: Yes

Testing: Yes

Colorado

Legal Option 1: Establish and operate a homeschool and file a notice of intent with the local superintendent.

Teacher qualifications: None

Subjects required: Yes

Record keeping: Maintain attendance records, test and evaluation results, and immunization records

Testing: Yes

or:

Enroll in a private school that allows home instruction.

Subjects required: Yes

Teacher qualifications: None

Record keeping: None

Testing: None

or:

Use a private tutor.

Teacher qualifications: Teacher certification

Subjects required: Yes

Record keeping: None

Testing: None

Connecticut

Establish and operate a home school.

Teacher qualifications: None

Subjects required: Yes

Record keeping: Parents maintain a portfolio indicating that instruction in the required courses has been given.

Testing: None

Delaware

Enroll in a home school association or organization that has registered with the Department of Education.

Teacher qualifications: None

Subjects required: Same as public schools

Record keeping: None

Testing: None

or:

Establish and operate a homeschool providing "regular and thorough instruction" to the satisfaction of the local superintendent and the state board of education, report enrollment, student ages, and attendance to the state department of education.

Teacher qualifications: None

Subjects required: Yes

Record keeping: None

Testing: Yes

District of Columbia

Provide private instruction not affiliated with an educational institution and provide notice of intent if the child is being removed from a public school.

Teacher qualifications: None

Subjects required: None

Record keeping: None

Testing: None

Florida

Establish and operate a homeschool and file a notice of intent with the local superintendent.

Teacher qualifications: None

Subjects required: None

Record keeping: Maintain a portfolio of records and materials

Testing: Yes

or:

Qualify and operate as part of a private school corporation (a legally incorporated group of homeschool families)

Teacher qualifications: None

Subjects required: None

Record keeping: None

Testing: None

Georgia

Establish and conduct a home study program and file a declaration of intent with the local superintendent.

Teacher qualifications: High school diploma or GED for a teaching parent; baccalaureate for any private tutor used

Subjects required: Yes

Record keeping: Maintain attendance records and submit monthly to the superintendent, and write and retain an annual progress report

Testing: Yes

Hawaii

Establish and operate a homeschool and file a notice of intent with the principal of the public school the child would otherwise be required to attend before starting to homeschool.

Teacher qualifications: None

Subjects required: None

Record keeping: Maintain a record of the planned curriculum.

Testing: Yes

or:

Enroll in a superintendent-approved appropriate alternative educational program.

Teacher qualifications: Baccalaureate degree

Subjects required: Yes
Record keeping: None
Testing: Yes

Idaho

Legal option: Provide an alternate educational experience for the child that "is otherwise comparably instructed."
Teacher qualifications: None
Subjects required: Yes
Record keeping: None
Testing: None

Illinois

Operate a homeschool as a private school.
Teacher qualifications: None
Subjects required: Yes
Record keeping: None
Testing: None

Indiana

Operate a homeschool as a private school and file a notice if required by the superintendent of education.
Teacher qualifications: None
Subjects required: None
Record keeping: Maintain attendance records
Testing: None

Iowa

Establish and operate a homeschool and complete an annual Competent Private Instruction Report Form; file two copies with the local school district.

Teacher qualifications: None

Subjects required: None

Record keeping: None

Testing: Yes

or:

Establish and operate a homeschool that is supervised by a licensed teacher and complete an annual Competent Private Instruction Form; file with the local school district.

Teacher qualifications: None for teaching parent; license for the supervising teacher

Subjects required: None

Record keeping: None

Testing: None

or:

Use a private tutor and complete an annual Competent Private Instruction Form; file with the local school district.

Teacher qualifications: Teaching license

Subjects required: None

Record keeping: None

Testing: None

Kansas

Operate a homeschool as a nonaccredited private school and register name and address of school with the state board of education.

Teacher qualifications: Must be a "competent" teacher

Subjects required: None

Record keeping: None

Testing: None

or: ·

Operate a homeschool as a satellite of an accredited private school

Teacher qualifications: Must be a "competent" teacher

Subjects required: Yes

Record keeping: As prescribed by the supervising private school

Testing: Yes

or:

Qualify for a state board of education–approved religious exemption in the high school grades.

Teacher qualifications: As prescribed during the approval process

Subjects required: Yes

Record keeping: As prescribed during the approval process

Testing: Yes

Kentucky

Qualify a homeschool as a private school and notify the local board of education of those students in attendance.

Teacher qualifications: None

Subjects required: Yes

Record keeping: Maintain an attendance register and scholarship reports

Testing: None

Louisiana

Establish and operate a homeschool as approved by the board of education and file an application and a copy of the child's birth certificate with the board of education.

Teacher qualifications: None

Subjects required: Yes

Record keeping: Submit with renewal application documents showing satisfactory evidence that the program is at least equal to that offered by the public schools

Testing: None

or:

Operate a homeschool as a private school and submit notification to the state department of education.

Teacher qualifications: None

Subjects required: Yes

Record keeping: None

Testing: None

Maine

Establish and operate a homeschool as approved by the local school board and the commissioner of the state department of education, and complete a state-provided Application for Equivalent Instruction through Home Instruction form; submit copies to the local school board and the state department of education.

Teacher qualifications: None

Subjects required: Yes

Record keeping: None

Testing: Yes

or:

Operate a homeschool as a nonapproved private school that teaches at least two unrelated students.

Teacher qualifications: None

Subjects required: None

Record keeping: None

Testing: None

Maryland

Establish and operate a qualified homeschool and file a notice of intent with the state department of education.

Teacher qualifications: None

Subjects required: Yes

Record keeping: None

Testing: None

or:

Provide supervised home instruction and file a notice of intent with the state department of education.

Teacher qualifications: None

Subjects required: Yes

Record keeping: As prescribed by the program
Testing: Yes

Massachusetts

Establish and operate a homeschool as approved in advance by the local school committee or superintendent.
Teacher qualifications: None
Subjects required: Yes
Record keeping: None
Testing: Yes

Michigan

Establish and operate a home education program.
Teacher qualifications: None
Subjects required: Yes
Record keeping: None
Testing: None
or:
Operate a homeschool as a nonpublic school and submit notice to the local superintendent.
Teacher qualifications: Teacher certification (unless claiming a religious exemption)
Subjects required: Yes
Record keeping: Maintain records of enrollment, courses of study, and qualifications of teachers (must be submitted to the Department of Education upon request)
Testing: None

Minnesota

Establish and operate a qualified homeschool and file with the local superintendent.

Teacher qualifications: None

Subjects required: Yes

Record keeping: If teaching parent is not at least a college graduate, submit a quarterly report to the local superintendent showing the achievement of each child in the required subjects

Testing: Yes

Mississippi

Establish and operate a homeschool and file a Certificate of Enrollment with the school district's attendance officer.

Teacher qualifications: None

Subjects required: None

Record keeping: None

Testing: None

Missouri

Establish and operate a homeschool.

Teacher qualifications: None

Subjects required: Yes

Record keeping: Maintain records of subjects taught, activities engaged in, samples of the child's academic work, and evaluations or a credible equivalent

Testing: None

Montana

Establish and operate a homeschool and file annual notice of intent with the county superintendent.

Teacher qualifications: None

Subjects required: Yes

Record keeping: Maintain attendance and immunization records, which must be available for inspection by county superintendent upon request.

Testing: None

Nebraska

Establish and operate a homeschool as a private school and file a notice of intent with the state commissioner.

Teacher qualifications: None, unless the teacher is "employed" by the family

Subjects required: Yes

Record keeping: None

Testing: None

Nevada

Establish and operate a homeschool and file with the local school board.

Subjects required: Yes

Teacher qualifications: (1) Possess a teaching certificate for grade level taught, or (2) consult with a licensed teacher or three-year homeschool veteran, or (3) use an approved correspondence course, or (4) obtain a waiver; options 1, 2, and 3 above are waived after first year

Record keeping: Must provide annual documentation to show that the child is receiving instruction equivalent to that approved by the state board of education

Testing: None

New Hampshire

Establish and operate a homeschool and file a notice of intent with a private school principal, the state commissioner of education, or the local superintendent.

Teacher qualifications: None

Subjects required: Yes

Record keeping: Maintain a portfolio of records and materials including a log of reading materials used, samples of writings, work sheets, or creative materials used or developed by the child

Testing: Yes

New Jersey

Establish and operate a homeschool.
Teacher qualifications: None
Subjects required: None
Record keeping: None
Testing: None

New Mexico

Establish and operate a homeschool and file notice of intent with the
school district.
Teacher qualifications: High school diploma or equivalent
Subjects required: Yes
Record keeping: Maintain attendance and immunization records
Testing: Yes

New York

Establish and operate a homeschool and file a notice of intent with the
local superintendent.
Teacher qualifications: "Competent"
Subjects required: Yes
Record keeping: Maintain attendance records (must make available for
inspection upon request of the local superintendent) and file with
the local superintendent quarterly reports listing the number of
hours of instruction during the quarter, description of material covered in each subject, and a grade or narrative evaluation in each subject
Testing: Yes

North Carolina

Establish and operate a homeschool and file a notice of intent with the
state division of nonpublic education.

Teacher qualifications: high school diploma or GED

Subjects required: None

Record keeping: Maintain attendance and immunization records and results of standardized tests

Testing: Yes

North Dakota

Establish and operate a homeschool and file an annual notice of intent with the local superintendent. For autistic children, in addition to above, file a copy of the child's diagnosis from a licensed psychologist along with an individualized education program developed and followed by the child's school district and parent or by a team selected and compensated by the parent.

Teacher qualifications: Possess (1) a teaching certificate, or (2) a baccalaureate degree, or (3) a high school diploma or GED and be monitored by a certified teacher during first two years or until child completes third grade, whichever is later; monitoring must continue thereafter if child scores below the 50th percentile on required standardized achievement test, or (4) proof of meeting or exceeding the cut-off score of the national teacher exam.

Subjects required: Yes

Record keeping: Maintain an annual record of courses and each child's academic progress assessments, including standardized achievement test results. For autistic children, also file with the local superintendent progress reports from an individualized education program team selected by the parent on or before November 1, February 1, and May 1 of each school year

Testing: Yes

or:

Operate a homeschool as a county- and state-approved private school.

Teacher qualifications: Teacher certification

Subjects required: Yes

Record keeping: None

Testing: None

Ohio

Establish and operate a homeschool and submit a notice of intent to the local superintendent.

Teacher qualifications: High school diploma, GED, test scores showing high school equivalence, or work under a person with a baccalaureate degree until child's test scores show proficiency or parent earns diploma or GED

Subjects required: Yes

Record keeping: None

Testing: Yes

Oklahoma

Establish and operate a homeschool as an "other means of education" expressed in the state constitution.

Teacher qualifications: None

Subjects required: Yes

Record keeping: None

Testing: None

Oregon

Establish and operate a homeschool and notify education service district in writing.

Teacher qualifications: None

Subjects required: None

Record keeping: None

Testing: Yes

Pennsylvania

Establish and operate a home education program and file a notarized affidavit with the local superintendent.

Teacher qualifications: High school diploma or equivalent

Subjects required: Yes

Record keeping: Maintain a portfolio of materials used, work done, standardized test results in grades three, five, and eight, and a written evaluation which must be completed each year

Testing: Yes

or:

Use a private tutor who: (1) is teaching one or more children who are members of a single family, (2) provides the majority of instruction, and (3) is receiving a fee or other consideration for instruction; file copy of certification and criminal history record with the local superintendent.

Teacher qualifications: Teacher certification

Subjects required: Yes

Record keeping: None

Testing: None

or:

Operate a homeschool as an extension or satellite of a private school and file a notarized affidavit with the department of education.

Teacher qualifications: None

Subjects required: Yes

Record keeping: None

Testing: None

Rhode Island

Establish and operate a homeschool as approved by the local school board.

Teacher qualifications: None

Subjects required: Yes

Record keeping: Maintain an attendance register

Testing: Yes

South Carolina

Establish and operate a homeschool as approved by the local school board.

Teacher qualifications: High school diploma or GED or a baccalaureate degree

Subjects required: Yes

Record keeping: Maintain evidence of regular instruction, including a record of subjects taught, activities in which the student and parent engage, a portfolio of the child's work, and a record of academic evaluations, with a semiannual progress report

Testing: Yes

or:

Establish and operate a homeschool under the membership auspices of the South Carolina Association of Independent Home Schools (SCAIHS).

Teacher qualifications: High school diploma or GED

Subjects required: Yes

Record keeping: None

Testing: None

or:

Establish and operate a homeschool under the membership auspices of an association for homeschools with no fewer than fifty members.

Teacher qualifications: High school diploma or GED

Subjects required: Yes

Record keeping: Maintain evidence of regular instruction, including a record of subjects taught, activities in which the student and parent engage, and a portfolio of the child's work, with a semiannual progress report

Testing: None

South Dakota

Establish and operate a homeschool and submit a notarized application to the local superintendent.

Teacher qualifications: None

Subjects required: Language arts and math

Record keeping: None

Testing: Yes

Tennessee

Establish and operate a homeschool and submit a notice of intent to the local superintendent.

Teacher qualifications: For grades K–8: High school diploma or GED. For grades 9–12:

College degree (or an exemption granted by the commissioner of education).

Subjects required: Yes

Record keeping: Maintain attendance records, which must be kept available for inspection and submitted to the local superintendent at the end the school year

Testing: Yes

or:

Establish and operate a homeschool in association with a church-related school, and for grades 9–12, register with the local school district each year.

Subjects required: As prescribed by the church-related school

Teacher qualifications: For grades K–8: High school diploma or GED; None for grades 9–12.

Record keeping: None

Testing: Yes

or:

Operate as a satellite campus of a church-related school.

Teacher qualifications: None

Subjects required: Yes

Record keeping: None

Testing: Yes

or:

Operate as a satellite campus of a nonrecognized religious school, based upon an assertion that the church-related school option unconstitutionally excludes certain religions.

Teacher qualifications: None

Subjects required: Yes

Record keeping: None
Testing: Yes

Texas

Establish and operate a homeschool as a private school.
Teacher qualifications: None
Subjects required: Yes
Record keeping: None
Testing: None

Utah

Establish and operate a homeschool as approved by the local school
board.
Teacher qualifications: None specified; however, the local school board
can consider the basic educative ability of the teacher.
Subjects required: Yes
Record keeping: None
Testing: None
or:
Establish a group of homeschool families as a regular private school.
Subjects required: None
Teacher qualification: None
Record keeping: None
Testing: None

Vermont

Establish and operate homeschool.
Teacher qualifications: None
Subjects required: Yes
Record keeping: None
Testing: Yes

Virginia

Establish and operate a homeschool and file an annual notice of intent with local superintendent.

Teacher qualifications: (1) Possess a baccalaureate degree, or (2) be a certified teacher, or (3) use an approved correspondence course, or (4) submit evidence parent can teach and use curriculum that includes state objectives for language arts and math

Subjects required: If operating under teacher qualification 4 above, math and language arts; for all others, none

Record keeping: None

Testing: Yes

or:

Operate a homeschool under the religious exemption statute.

Teacher qualifications: None

Subjects required: None

Record keeping: None

Testing: None

or:

Use a private tutor and file a notice of intent with the local superintendent.

Teacher qualifications: Teacher certification

Subjects required: None

Record keeping: None

Testing: None

Washington

Establish and operate a homeschool and file a notice of intent with the local (or applicable nonresident) superintendent.

Teacher qualifications: (1) Be supervised by a certified teacher, or (2) have 45 college quarter credit hours or complete a course in home education, or (3) be deemed qualified by the local superintendent

Subjects required: Yes

Record keeping: Maintain standardized test scores, academic progress assessments, and immunization records

Testing: Yes

West Virginia

Seek local school board approval to operate a homeschool.

Teacher qualifications: Be deemed qualified to teach by the local super-intendent and school board

Subjects required: Yes

Record keeping: As prescribed during the approval process

Testing: Yes

or:

Establish and operate a homeschool and file a notice of intent with the local superintendent.

Subjects required: Yes

Record keeping: None

Testing: Yes

Wisconsin

Establish and operate a "home-based private educational program" and file a statement of enrollment with the state department of education.

Teacher qualifications: None

Subjects required: Yes

Record keeping: None

Testing: None

Wyoming

Notice: Annually submit to the local school board a curriculum showing that a "basic academic educational program" is being provided.

Teacher qualifications: None

Subjects required: Yes

Record keeping: None

Testing: None

Homeschool Organizations

**Home School Legal Defense
Association**
P.O. Box 3000
Purcellville, VA 20134
(540) 338-5600
www.hslda.org

Adventist Home Educator
P.O. Box 836
Camino, CA 95709-0836
(916) 647-2110
www.adventtech.com/ahe

Jewish Home Educator's Network
c/o koenig
409 North Broad
Carlinville, IL 62626
beithoro@erols.com
http://snj.com/jhen

**National Association for Mormon
Home Educators**
2770 South 1000 West
Perry, UT 84302

**National Association of Catholic
Home Educators**
P.O. Box 787
Montrose, AL 36559
http://www.nache.com

**National Handicapped
Homeschoolers Association**
5383 Alpine Road. SE
Oglalla, WA 98359
Tom and Sherry Bushnell: (206) 857-
4257

**National Home Education
Research Institute**
P.O. Box 13939
Salem, OR 97309
(503) 364-1490
http://www.nheri.org

**Native American Homeschool
Association**
P.O. Box 979
Fries, VA 24330
(540) 744-3640
http://www.expage.com/page/
nahomeschool

Rutherford Institute
P.O. Box 7482
Charlottesville, VA 22906
(804) 978-3888

Alliance for Parental Involvement in Education
P.O. Box 59
East Chatham, NY 12060-0059
Seth Rockmuller or Kathryn Houk
(518) 392-6900
allpie@taconic.net
http://www.croton.com/allpie

Alternative Education Resource Organization
417 Roslyn Road
Roslyn Heights, NY 11577
Jerry Mintz (516) 621-2195
JMintz@igc.acp.com

American Homeschool Association
P.O. Box 3142
Palmer, AK 99645
AHA@home-ed-magazine.com
http://www.home-ed-magazine.com/
AHA/aha.html

Family Unschoolers Network
1688 Belhaven Woods Court
Pasadena, MD 21122-3727
FUN@IQCweb.com
http://www.IQCweb.com/fun

Holt Associates
2380 Massachusetts Avenue,
Suite 104
Cambridge, MA 02140
(617) 864-3100
HoltGWS@erols.com
http://www.holtgws.com

Moore Foundation
P.O. Box 1
Camas, WA 98607
(360) 835-2736
moorefnd@pacifier.com
http://www.caslink.com/
moorefoundation

National Homeschool Association
P.O. Box 290
Heartland, MI 48353
(513) 772-9580
http://www.n-h-a.org

State Support Groups and Organizations

Alabama

Alabama Home Educators Network (AHEN)
3015 Thurman Road
Huntsville, AL 35805
Lisa Bugg (205) 534-6401
KaeKaeB@aol.com
http://members.aol.com/haekaeb/
ahen.html

**Christian Home Education
Fellowship of AL (CHEF)**
816 Colonial Drive
Alabaster, AL 35007
(205) 664-2232

**Home Educators of Alabama
Round Table (HEART)**
http://www.heartofalabama.org

Alaska

Alaska Homeschoolers Association
P.O. Box 230973
Anchorage, AK 99504-3527

Arizona

**Arizona Families for Home
Education**
P.O. Box 4661
Scottsdale, AZ 85261-4661
(800) 929-3927

**Phoenix Learning Alternatives
Network**
Nancy Sherr (602) 483-3381

TELAO Home Educators
4700 North Tonalea Trail
Tuscan, AZ 85749
(520) 749-4757

Arkansas

**Arkansas Christian Home
Educators Association (ACHEA)**
P.O. Box 4025
North Little Rock, AR 72190
(501) 758-9099

**Home Educators of Arkansas
(HEAR)**
Coalition of Arkansas Parents (CAP)
P.O. Box 192455
Little Rock, AR 72219
http://bucket.ualr.edu/~sort/cap.html

**Home Educators of Arkansas
Voicing Excellence Now
(HEAVEN)**
8 Glenbrook Place
Sherwood, AR 72120

California

**California Homeschool Network
(CHN)**
P.O. Box 55485
Hayward, CA 94545
(800) 327-5339
CHNMail@aol.com
http://www.comenius.org/
   chnpage.htm

Central California Homeschoolers
7600 Marchant
Atascadero, CA 93422
Barbara Alward (805) 462-0726

**Christian Home Educators
Association of California**
P.O. Box 2009
Norwalk, CA 90651-2009
(800) 564-2432

**Homefires Journal of
Homeschooling**
180 El Camino Real, Suite 10
Millbrae, CA 94030
(888) 4-HOME-ED
editor@homefires.com
http://www.Homefires.com

**HomeSchool Association of
California**
P.O. Box 2442
Atascadero, CA 93423
(888) 472-4440
info@hsc.org
http://www.hsc.org

Colorado

Boulder County Home Educators
1495 Riverside
Boulder, CO 80304
Valerie Berg (303) 449-5916

**Christian Home Educators of
Colorado**
3739 East 4th Avenue
Denver, CO 80206
(303) 388-1888
http://www.learnathome.com/chec/
    index.htm

**Colorado Home Educator's
Association**
3043 South Laredo Circle
Aurora, CO 80013
(303) 441-9938
pinewood@dash.com

**Rocky Mountain Education
Connection (RMEC)**
20774 East Buchanan Drive
Aurora, CO 80011
(303) 341-2242
connect@pcisys.net
http://www.pcisys.net/~dstanley

Connecticut

**Connecticut Home Educators
Association**
80 Coppermine Road
Oxford, CT 06478
Mary Beth Nelson: (203) 732-0102

**CT's CURE (CT's Citizens to
Uphold the Right to Educate)**
P.O. Box 597
Sherman, CT 06784
Alison Brion (203) 355-4724

**The Education Association of
Christian Homeschoolers
(TEACH)**
25 Field Stone Run
Farmington, CT 06032
(800) 205-8744
http://www.tiac.net/users/
    bobpers/teach

Unschoolers Support
22 Wildrose Avenue
Guilford, CT 06437
Luz Shosie (203) 458-7402

Delaware

Delaware Home Education Association
P.O. Box 1003
Dover, DE 19903
(302) 429-0515

Tri-State Home School Network
P.O. Box 7193
Newark, DE 19714-7193
(302) 322-2018

Florida

The Family Learning Exchange
2020 Turpentine Road
Mims, FL 32754
(407) 268-8833

Florida Parent Educators Association
P.O. Box 371
Melbourne, FL 32902-1193
(407) 722-0895
office@FPEA.com
http://www.fpea.com

Home Education Resources and Information
711 St. Johns Bluff Road
Jacksonville, FL 32225
(904) 565-9121
herijax@juno.com

Home Educators Assistance League
3343 Shoal Creek Cove
Crestview, FL 32539
Carri Bundy (904) 682-2422

Home Educators Lending Parents Support
5941 Northwest 14 Court
Sunrise, FL 33313
Susie Capraro (954) 791-9733
Scapraro-helps@juno.com

The Homeschool Network
P.O. Box 940402
Maitland, FL 32794
Lyn Milum (407) 889-4632
gorest5@gdi.net

Georgia

Atlanta Alternative Education Network
1586 Rainier Falls Drive
Atlanta, GA 30329
(404) 636-6348
http://www.mindspring.com/~lei/
aaen

Free To Learn At Home
4439 Lake Forest Drive
Oakwood, GA 30566
(770) 536-8077

Georgia Home Education Association
245 Buckeye Lane
Fayetteville, GA 30214
(770) 461-3657

Georgians for Freedom in Education
7189 Cane Leaf Drive
Fairburn, GA 30213
Billie Jean Bryant (770) 463-1563

LIGHT
P.O. Box 2724
Columbus, GA 31902
(706) 324-3714

Hawaii

Christian Home Educators of Hawaii
91-824 Oama Street
Ewa Beach, HI 96706
(808) 689-6398
CHOHALOHA@aol.com
http://www.maui.net/~madelein/
chem-news.html

Hawaii Homeschool Association
P.O. Box 3476
Mililani, HI 96789
(808) 944-3339
TGthrngPlc@aol.com

Idaho

Family Unschooling Network
1809 North 7th Street
Boise, ID 83702
(208) 345-2703
NeysaJensen@compuserve.com

Idaho Home Educators
P.O. Box 1324
Meridian, ID 83680
(208) 323-0230

Palouse Home Learning Alternatives
802 White Avenue
Moscow, ID 83843
Peg Harvey (208) 882-1593

Illinois

Home Oriented Unique Schooling Experience (HOUSE)
2508 East 22nd Place
Sauk Village, IL 60411
Teresa Sneade (708) 758-7374
http://www.geocities.com/athens/
acropolis/7804

Illinois Christian Home Educators
P.O. Box 261
Zion, IL 60099
(847) 328-7129
http://user.aol.com/ilchec

Unschoolers Network
736 North Metchell Avenue
Arlington Heights, IL 60004
PJADK@aol.com

Indiana

Families Learning Together
1714 East 51st Street
Indianapolis, IN 46205
(317) 255-9298
whelan.mullen@juno.com

Homefront
1120 West Whiskey Run Road
New Salisbury, IN 47161-8823
Donnell and Teresa Royer
(812) 347-2931

Indiana Association of Home Educators
1000 North Madison
Greenwood, IN 46142
(317) 638-9633

L.E.A.R.N.
Barbara Benson
9577 East State Road 45
Unionville, IN 47468
(812) 336-8028

Wabash Valley Homeschool Association
P.O. Box 3865
Terre Haute, IN 47803
WVHA@aol.com

Iowa

Network of Iowa Christian Home Educators
P.O. Box 158
Dexter, IA 50070
(800) 723-0438

Rebecca Leach
2301 South Henry Street
Sioux City, IA 51106
(712) 274-0472
Beckyleach@aol.com

Kansas

Circle of Homeschoolers and Unschoolers in Central Kansas Learning Eclectically (CHUCKLE)
Rural Route 1, Box 28A
Rush Center, KS 67575
Susan Peach: (913) 372-4457

Christian Home Educators Confederation of Kansas
P.O. Box 3968
Wichita, KS 66203
(913) 234-2927

Heartland Area Homeschoolers' Association
823 West Street
Emporia, KS 66801
Shiuvaun Sowder: (316) 343-3696

Lawrence Area Unaffiliated Group of Homeschoolers (LAUGH)
Rural Route 1, Box 496
Perry, KS 66073
Barbara Michener: (913) 597-5579

Kentucky

Bluegrass Home Educators
600 Shake Rag Road
Waynesburg, KY 40489
KyHomeEd@mis.net
http://www.BluegrassHmEd.nvo.com

Christian Home Educators of Kentucky
691 Howardstown Road
Hodgensville, KY 42748
(502) 358-9270

Kentucky Home Education Association
P.O. Box 81
Winchester, KY 40392-0081

Kentucky Independent Learners Network
P.O. Box 275
Somerset, KY 42501
Meg McClory (606) 678-2527

Louisiana

Christian Home Education Fellowship of Louisiana
P.O. Box 74292
Baton Rouge, LA 70874-4292
(504) 775-9709

Homeschoolers Learning from Mother Earth
14189 Ridge Road
Prairieville, LA 70769
Roxann Phillips (504) 673-8367

Louisiana Home Education Network (LAHEN)
http://members.aol.com/LaHomeED/
    Lahen.html

Wild Azalea Homeschoolers
6055 General Meyer Avenue
New Orleans, LA 70131
Tracey Sherry (504) 392-5647
tws01@gnofn.org

Maine

Homeschool Support Network
P.O. Box 708
Gray, ME 04039
Jane Boswell (207) 657-2800
hsn@outrig.com
http://www.chfweb.com/hsn

Homeschoolers of Maine
HC 62, Box 24
Hope, ME 04847
(207) 763-4251

Maine Home Education Association
P.O. Box 421
Popsham, ME 04086
(800) 520-0577

Southern Maine Home Education Support Network
76 Beech Ridge Road
Scarborough, ME 04074
Eileen Yoder (207) 883-9621

Maryland

Christian Home Educators Network
P.O. Box 2010
Elliscott City, MD 21043
(410) 744-8919

Maryland Association of Christian Home Educators
P.O. Box 247
Point of Rock, MD 21777-0247
(301) 607-4284

Maryland Home Education Association
9085 Flamepool Way
Columbia, MD 21045
Manfred W. Smith (410) 730-0073

North County Home Educators
1688 Belhaven Woods Court
Pasadena, MD 21122-3727
Billy or Nancy Greer (410) 437-5109
NCHE@IQCweb.com
http://www.IQCweb.com/fun/
    nche.htm

Massachusetts

Massachusetts Home Learning Association
P.O. Box 1558
Marstons Mills, MA 02648
Loretta Heuer (508) 376-1923
Kathy Smith (508) 249-9056
http://horthshore.shore.net/~pyghill/
   mhla.htm

Massachusetts Homeschool Organization of Parent Educators (Mass HOPE)
5 Atwood Road
Cherry Valley, MA 01611-3332
(508) 755-4754

Michigan

Christian Home Educators of Michigan
P.O. Box 2357
Farmington Hills, MI 48333
(810) 683-3395

Families Learning and Schooling at Home (FLASH)
21671 B Drive North
Marshall, MI 49068
Natalie Valle (616) 781-1069

Heritage Home Educators
2122 Houser
Holly, MI 48442

Hillsdale Area Homeschoolers
5151 Barker Road
Jonesville, MI 49250
Linda Kline (517) 287-5565

Home Educators Circle
1280 John Hix Street
Westland, MI 48186
(313) 326-5406

Information Network for Christian Homes (INCH)
4934 Cannonsburg Road
Belmont, MI 49306
(616) 874-5656

Minnesota

Minnesota Association of Christian Home Educators
P.O. Box 32308
Fridley, MN 55432-0308
(612) 717-9070

Minnesota Homeschoolers Alliance
P.O. Box 23072
Richfield, MN 55423
(612) 491-2828

Mississippi

Coast Military Home Educators
9212A Givens Circle
Biloxi, MS 39531
Lori & John Hudson (601) 388-4522

Home Educators of Central Mississippi
535 Luling Street
Pearl, MS 39208
601-978-2204

Mississippi Home Educators Association
109 Reagan Ranch Road
Laurel, MS 39440
(601) 649-6432

Missouri

Missouri Association of Teaching Christian Homes
307 East Ash Street, #146
Columbia, MO 65201
(573) 443-8217

Ozark Lore Society
HC 73, Box 160
Drury, MO 65638
Debra Eisenmann (417) 679-3391
deb@wiseheart.com

St. Louis Homeschooling Network
4147 East Pine
St. Louis, MO 63108
Karen Karabel (314) 534-1171

Montana

Independent Homeschoolers Network of Bozeman
415 South Ninth Avenue
Bozeman, MT 59715
Katie Perry (406) 586-4564

Mid-Mountain Home Education Network
P.O. Box 2182
Montana City Station
Clancy, MT 59634
Karen Semple (406) 443-3376

Montana Coalition of Home Educators
P.O. Box 43
Gallatin Gateway, MT 59730
(406) 587-6163

Nebraska

LEARN
7741 East Avon Lane
Lincoln, NE 68505-2043
Rose Yonekura (402) 488-7741

New Hampshire

Christian Home Educators of New Hampshire
P.O. Box 961
Manchester, NH 03105-0916
(603) 569-2343

Homeschooling Friends
204 Brackett Road
New Durham, NH 03855
Beverly Behr (603) 332-4146
nothome@worldpath.net
http://web-enrichment.com/hsf/

New Hampshire Alliance for Home Education
17 Preseve Drive
Nashua, NH 03060
Betsey Westgate (603) 880-8629

New Hampshire Homeschooling Coalition
P.O. Box 2224
Concord, NH 03304-2224
Abbey Lawrence (603) 539-7233

New Jersey

Education Network of Christian Homeschoolers of New Jersey
65 Middlesex Road
Matawan, NJ 07747
(908) 583-7128

Homeschoolers of South New Jersey
1239 Whitaker Avenue
Millville, NJ 08332
(609) 327-1224
Tutor@Pulsar.net
http://www.pulsar.net/~tutor

Unschooler's Network
2 Smith Street
Farmingdale, NJ 07727
Nancy Plent (732) 938-2473

Unschooling Families Support Group of Central New Jersey
150 Folwell Station Road
Jobstown, NJ 08041
Karen Mende-Fridkis (609) 723-1524

New Mexico

Christian Association of Parent Educators
P.O. Box 25046
Albuquerque, NM 87125
(505) 898-8548

New Mexico Family Educators
P.O. 92276
Albuquerque, NM 87199-2276
(505) 275-7053

Unschoolers of Albuquerque
8505 Bellrose NE
Albuquerque, NM 87111
Barbara Dawson (505) 275-0422
Sandra Dodd (505) 299-2476
SandraDodd@aol.com

New York

Families for Home Education
3219 Coulter Road
Cazenovia, NY 13035
Peg Moore (315) 655-2574

Fingerlakes Unschoolers Network
201 Elm Street
Ithaca, NY 14850
Clare Grady (607) 273-6257
Laundress@aol.com

Loving Education at Home (LEAH)
P.O. Box 88
Cato, NY 13033
(716) 346-0939
http://www.leah.org

New York City Home Educators Alliance
8 East 2nd Street
New York, NY 10156
(212) 505-9884
Rtricamo@aol.com

New York State Home Education News
P.O. Box 59
East Chatham, NY 12060
Seth Rockmuller or Katherine Houk
(518) 392-6900

Oneida Lake Area Home Educators
P.O. Box 24
Sylvan Beach, NY 13157
Chris Wheeler (315) 762-5166

Oneonta Area Sharing In Homeschooling (OASIS)
P.O. Box 48
Gilbertsville, NY 13776
Darlene Abajian (607) 783-2271

Tri-County Homeschoolers
P.O. Box 190
Ossining, NY 10562
Chris and Andy Hofer (914) 941-5607
chofer@croton.com
http://www.croton.com/home-ed

Tri-Lakes Community Home Educators
P.O. Box 270
Raybrook, NY 12977
Lynn Waickman (518) 891-5657
Royce Cano (518) 796-4840

North Carolina

Families Learning Together
1670 NC Highway 33W
Chocowinity, NC 27817

North Carolinians for Home Education
419 North Boylan Avenue
Raleigh, NC 27603-1211
Susan Van Dyke (919) 834-6243

North Dakota

North Dakota Home School Association
4007 North State Street
Bismarck, ND 58501
(701) 223-4080

Ohio

Association of Ohio Homeschoolers
3636 Paris Boulevard
Westerville, OH 43081

Parents and Children Together (PACT)
8944 Weiss Road
Union City, OH 45390
(927) 692-5680

Oklahoma

Christian Home Educators Fellowship of Oklahoma
P.O. Box 471363
Tulsa, OK 74147
(918) 583-7323

Home Educators Resource Organization (HERO) of Oklahoma
302 North Coolidge
Enid, OK 73703
Leslie Moyer (580) 438-2253
mjmiller@pldi.ne
http://www.geocites.com/Athens/Forum/3236

Oregon

Oregon Christian Home Education Association Network
2815 NE 37th
Portland, OR 97212
(508) 288-1285

Oregon Home Education Network (OHEN)
4470 SW Hall Boulevard, #286
Beaverton, OR 97005
Jeanne Biggerstaff (503) 321-5166
sassenak@teleport.com
http://www.teleport.com/~ohen/

Greater Portland Homeschoolers
P.O. Box 82415
Portland, OR 97282
Kathy Schertz (503) 241-5350
Schertzkat@aol.com

Pennsylvania

Christian Homeschool Association of Pennsylvania (CHAP)
P.O. Box 3603
York, PA 17402-0603
(717) 661-2428

Pennsylvania Home Education Network (PHEN)
285 Allegheny Street
Meadville, PA 16355
Kathy Terleski (412) 561-5288

Pennsylvania Home Education News
P.O. Box 305
Summerhill, PA 15958
Karen Leventry (814) 495-5651
Karenleven@aol.com

Rhode Island

Rhode Island Guild of Home Teachers (RIGHT)
P.O. Box 11
Hope, RI 02831
(401) 821-7700
right_right@mailexcite.com
http://www.angelfire.com/ri/RIGHT

South County Homeschoolers
500 Carolina Back Road
Charleston, RI 02813

South Carolina

Home Organization of Parent Educators
1697 Dotterer's Run
Charleston, SC 29414
(803) 763-7833
epeeler@awod.com

South Carolina Association of Independent Home Schools (SCAIHS)
P.O. Box 2104
Irmo, SC 29063
(803) 551-1003

South Carolina Homeschool Alliance
1679 Memorial Park Road, Suite 179
Lancaster, SC 29720
ConnectSC@aol.com
http://members.aol.com/connectsc

South Dakota

South Dakota Home School Association
P.O. Box 882
Sioux Falls, SD 57101-0882
Kim Liedtke (605) 338-9689

Western Dakota Christian Home Schools
P.O. Box 528
Black Hawk, SD 57718
(605) 923-1893

Tennessee

State of Franklin Homeschoolers
494 Mill Creek Road
Kingsport, TN 37664
(423) 349-6125
kramerbg@mounet.com

Tennessee Home Education Association
3677 Richbriar Court
Nashville, TN 37211
(615) 834-3529

Tennessee Homeschooling Families
214 Park Lane
Oliver Springs, TN 37840
Lin Kemper Wallace (423) 435-9644

Unschoolers of Memphis
Margaret Meyer (901) 757-9859

Texas

Home-Oriented Private Education
P.O. Box 59876
Dallas, TX 75229
(972) 358-2221

North Texas Self-Educators
150 Forest Lane
Double Oak/Lewisville, TX 75067
Sarah Jordan (817) 430-4835

South Texas Self-Learners
1005 Delta Drive
Corpus Christi, TX 78412
Becky Davis (512) 992-7549

Texas Home School Coalition
P.O. Box 6982
Lubbock, TX 79493
(806) 797-4927

Texas Advocates for Freedom in Education (TAFFIE)
13635 Greenridge Street
Sugar Land, TX 77478
Beth Jackson (713) 242-7994

Utah

Latter-Day Saint Home Educators' Association
2770 South 1000 West
Perry, UT 84302
Joyce Kinmont (801) 723-5355

Utah Christian Homeschoolers
P.O. Box 3942
Salt Lake City, UT 84110
(801) 255-4053

Utah Home Education Association
P.O. Box 167
Roy, UT 84067
(888) 887-UHEA
http://sss.itsnet.com/~uhea

Vermont

Center for Homeschooling
95 North Avenue
Burlington, VT 05401
Deb Shell (802) 862-9616

Christian Home Education of Vermont
214 North Prospect, #105
Burlington, VT 05401
(802) 658-4561

Vermont Homeschoolers' Association
Rural Route 2, Box 4440
Bristol, VT 05443
(802) 453-5460

Virginia

Community of Independent Learners
P.O. Box 16029
Alexandria, VA 22302

Home Educators Association of Virginia
1900 Byrd Avenue, Suite 201
P.O. Box 6745
Richmond, VA 23230-0745
(804) 288-1608

Virginia Home Education Association
1612 Columbia Road
Gordonsville, VA 22942
(540) 832-3578
vhea@virginia.edu
http://poe.acc.virginia.edu/~pm6f/
   vhea.html

Washington

Family Learning Organization
P.O. Box 7247
Spokane, WA 99207-0247
Kathleen McCurdy (509) 467-2552

Homeschoolers' Support Association
P.O. Box 413
Maple Valley, WA 98038
Teresa Sparling (206) 746-5047

Teaching Parents Association
P.O. Box 1934
Woodinville, WA 98072-1934
Meriann Roberts (206) 788-5272
Janice Kugler (206) 821-2753

Washington Association of Teaching Christian Homes
2904 North Dora Road
Spokane, WA 99212
(509) 922-4811

Washington Homeschool Organization
18130 Midvale Avenue North,
   Suite C
Seattle, WA 98133
(206) 298-8942

West Virginia

Christian Home Educators of West Virginia
P.O. Box 8770
South Charleston, WV 25303-8770
(304) 776-4664

West Virginia Home Educators Association
P.O. Box 3707
Charleston, WV 25337
(800) 736-WVHE
wvhea@bigfoot.com
http://members.tripod.com/
~WVHEA

Wisconsin

H.O.M.E.
5745 Bittersweet Place
Madison, WI 53705
Alison McKee (608) 238-3302

Wisconsin Christian Home Educators Association
2307 Carmel Avenue
Racine, WI 53405
(414) 637-5127

Wisconsin Parents Association
P.O. Box 2502
Madison, WI 53701-2502

Wyoming

Homeschoolers of Wyoming
339 Bicentennial Court
Powell, WY 82435
(307) 754-3271

Unschoolers of Wyoming
Laramie Home Education Network
429 Hwy 230, #20
Laramie, WY 82010

Homeschool Product Suppliers

A Beka Home Book
P.O. Box 19100
Pensacola, FL 32523-9100
1-877-223-5226
www.abeka.org

A Beka sells complete curricula for all grades and also sells the various subjects individually.

Animal Town
P.O. Box 757
Greenland, NH 03840
1-800-445-8642
Fax 1-603-430-0334
www.animaltown.com

Animal Town features noncompetitive and educational games, art sets and craft kits, and items needed for outdoor fun like kites, sack-race sacks, a children's croquet set, scooters, and more.

Barnum Educational Software
3450 Lake Shore Avenue, Suite 200
Oakland, CA 94610
800-553-9155/510-465-5070 (Outside U.S./Canada)
Fax: 800-553-9156/510-465-5071 (Outside U.S./Canada)
www.thequartermile.com

A source for The Quarter Mile Math program.

Barron's Educational Series, Inc.
250 Wireless Blvd.
Hauppauge, NY, 11788
1-800-645-3476
Fax 1-631-434-3723
www.barronseduc.com

A source for many textbooks and supplements for a variety of school subjects, including the Easy Way Series.

The Book Peddler's Wares
P.O. Box 1960
Elyria, OH 44036-1960
1-800-928-1760
1-440-284-6654
Fax 1-440-323-9494
www.the-book-peddler.com

This catalogue has a variety of curricula materials and books about homeschooling. The Book Peddler has a particularly strong literature selection.

Building Thinking Skills
P.O. Box 448
Pacific Grove, CA 93950-0448
1-800-458-4849
Fax 831-393-3277
www.criticalthinking.com

Building Thinking Skills offers resources such as the Cranium Crackers and Reading Detective series that are designed to develop problem-solving skills.

CBD Home School
Christian Book Distributors
P.O. Box 7000
Peabody, MA 01961-7000
1-800-247-4784 US and Canada
1-978-977-5005 All other countries
Fax 1-978-977-5010
www.christianbook.com
orders@christianbook.com

The CD catalogue offers a large selection of educational resources, including many specifically for Christians. It is a source for Miquon Math, the Key To . . . series of math workbooks, Saxon Math, Alpha Omega Curricula, Bob Jones Curricula, Pimsleur Language programs, Power Glide programs, The Learnables, and much more.

Chalk Dust Company

11 Sterling Court
Sugar Land, TX 77479
Ph: 281-265-2495
800-588-7564
www.chalkdust.com

This is the home of the Chalk Dust math video programs.

Chinaberry

Suite B
2780 Via Orange Way
Spring Valley, CA 91978
1-800-776-2242
Fax-619-670-5203
www.Chinaberry.com

The Chinaberry catalogue has books for all ages, stories on cassette and CD, and some miscellaneous goodies like craft kits and gorgeous silk wings that children can wear to play angels or butterflies.

Each book has a detailed description that makes it especially helpful in choosing books for children. According to the catalogue, "Chinaberry offers items to support families in raising their children with love, honesty, and joy to be reverent, loving caretakers of each other and the earth."

Classroom Direct.com

P.O. Box 830677
Birmingham, AL 35283-0677
1-800-599-3040
Fax 1-800-628-6250
www.classroomdirect.com

This is a huge catalogue with over 400 pages of the sorts of items usually found in school supply stores. There are books and games and activities for teaching all the typical school subjects. It includes easels and chalkboards and furniture for the classroom. Classroom Direct.com guarantees that its prices cannot be beat, and prices are even lower when the items are ordered from its website.

Edmund Scientific Company

Gloucester Pike
Barrington, NJ 08007-1380

A large selection of science resources.

The Education Connection

Box 910367
St. George, UT 84791
1-800-863-3828
Fax 1-800-227-6609
www.educationconnection.com

The Education Connection offers homeschooling books, curricula materials, learning games, and more. It sells Daily G.R.A.M.S., Bob Books, Math-It, Menu Math, The Phonics Game, and much more.

ETA/Cuisenaire500

Greenview Court
Vernon Hills, IL 60061
800-445-5985 or 847-816-5050
Fax: 800-875-9643 or 847-816-5066
www.etacuisenaire.com

A source for Cuisenaire rods and much more.

Farm Country General Store

412 North Fork Rd.
Metamora, IL 61548
309-367-2844
fcgs@mtco.com
www.homeschoolfcgs.com

This is a large catalogue packed with a variety of books and curricula for the homeschooling family. It is a source for The New Learning Language Arts Through Literature, Writing Strands, Wordsmith, Saxon Math, McGuffey Readers, Five In a Row unit studies, and the

Yellow Pages for Students and Teachers Series, just to name a few. It also has Christian resources.

Friendship House
Suite G
29313 Clemens Road
P.O. Box 450978
Cleveland, OH 44145-0623
1-800-791-9876
www.friendshiphouse.com
Fax 1-440-871-0858

This is a catalogue of resources for teaching music theory; also has music-related gifts.

Greenleaf Press
Unit D
3761 Hwy. 109 North
Lebannon, TN 37087
615-449-1617
orders@greenleafpress.com

Greenleaf is well known among homeschoolers for its history resources and also sells general homeschooling books.

Hands ON and Beyond
4813 East Marshall Dr.
Vestal, NY 13850
1-888-20-LEARN
www.HandsOnAndBeyond.com

This catalogue has hands-on science kits, an assortment of American Girl books, Saxon Math, Power Glide language programs, and much more.

Hands-On Science
Delta Education
P.O. Box 3000
Nashua, NH 03061-3000
1-800-442-5444
Fax 1-800-282-9560
www.delta-education.com

This catalogue has treasures such as owl pellets and vermin-composting kits with earthworms. It has a variety of microscopes, National Geographic videos, and items needed to explore magnetism, light, electricity, weather, and many other topics.

John Holt's Bookstore
P.O. Box 8006
Walled Lake, MI 48391-8006
617-864-3100
holtgws@erols.com
www.holtgws.com

This catalogue, as well as the magazine, *Growing Without Schooling* is produced by Holt Associates. John Holt was a pioneer in the homeschooling movement and a proponent of the "unschooling" approach in particular. The catalogue sells quite a few general homeschooling books, in addition to its unschooling resources.

The Home School
P.O. Box 308
North Chelmsford, MA 01863-0308
www.thehomeschool.com
1-800-788-1221

Key Curriculum Press
P.O. Box 2304
Berkeley, CA 94702
1-800-995-MATH

Publishes the Key To . . . math workbook series, and also Miquon Math materials.

Love to Learn
741 N. State Road
Salem, UT 84653
1-801-423-2009
1-888-771-1034
Fax 1-801-423-9188
email orders@LoveToLearn.net
http://www.LoveToLearn.net

This catalogue has a variety of books, workbooks, games, and puzzles to help teach the usual school subjects and more. It has a selection of items to keep preschoolers and toddlers busy while their parent is working with the older siblings. It also has Christian resources, including Bible action figures!

MindWare
121 5th Avenue NW
New Brighton, MN 55112
1-800-999-0398
www.MINDWAREonline.com

Toys and games that make kids and adults use their brains.

Music for Little People
P.O. Box 757
Greenland, NH 03840
1-800-409-2457
www.mflp.com

Music for Little People has a large selection of children's music on cassette, CD, and video, as well as musical instruments and kits for projects like tie-dying and making bead bracelets.

Saxon Publishers, Inc.
2450 John Saxon Blvd.
Norman, OK 73071
1-800-284-7019
405-329-7071
www.saxonpub.com

Here is a source for the Saxon Math curriculum.

Timberdoodle
1510 E. Spencer Lake Road
Shelton, WA 98584
360-426-0672
www.timberdoodle.com

A variety of homeschool supplies. This catalogue is run by a homeschooling family, and they explain their recommendations for the products they carry.

Tobin's Lab
P.O. Box 725
Culpepper, VA 22701
1-800-522-4776
mike@tobinlab.com
www.tobinlab.com

Tobin's Lab offers a wide assortment of hands-on science materials and books.

World of Reading, LTD
P.O. Box 13092
Atlanta, GA 30324-0092
404-233-4042; 1-800-729-3703
Fax 404-237-5511
polyglot@wor.com
www.wor.com

This is a large catalogue devoted exclusively to resources for learning foreign languages . . . over 100 of them!

Young Explorers, LLC
1810 W. Eisenhower Blvd.
P.O. Box 2257
Loveland, CO 80539
1-888-928-3285 or 1-800-239-7577
Fax: 1-888-876-8847
www.youngexplorers.com

Toys and games that challenge the mind and foster creativity.

Useful Websites

General Homeschool Websites

www.planethomeschool.com   This is our homeschool website, and it is chock full of information for the new homeschooler, homeschooling parents, and children. With an incredible amount of content, hands-on projects, educational programs, chat rooms, bulletin boards, interactive games, links to everything you could dream of, and a soon-to-be-added curriculum swap shop, this site may be all the homeschooler needs!

www.homeschoolzone.com

www.homeschooling.about.com

www.fun-books.com/homeschooling.htm

www.gomilpitas.com/homeschooling   Has a lot of resources for homeschooling.

www.home-school.com/   Official website of practical homeschooling magazine.

www.midnightbeach.com/hs

theswap.com   Buy, sell, and trade used homeschooling books and supplies. Has a writing showcase for all ages. Also contains a variety of message boards.

www.kaleidoscapes.com   Has message boards where you can discuss curricula and all kinds of stuff related to homeschooling. This site has some really neat kids' pages. One has a kids' animations page. Animations are posted on display for a couple of weeks afterwards!

www.lessonplanspage.com Lots of free lesson plans.

Encyclopedias

There's no need to invest a small fortune in encyclopedias when you can access them for free online! Some of the sites charge a small fee for access, but you'd be surprised at how much access you can gain for free! Check them out!

www.britannica.com   Encyclopedia Britannica has an awesome Internet Guide as well as a wealth of encyclopedic information.

www.encyclopedia.com

www.encarta.msn.com/EncartaHome.asp

worldbook.com

With these three sites you should be able to find any encyclopedic information you need!

www.cs.uh.edu/~clifton/micro.a.html This site helps by categorizing the Internet so that it functions like one giant encyclopedia.

Dictionaries

www.dictionary.com

www.vocabulary.com

www.m-w.com

www.bartleby.com/62/

Webster's even has a "word for the day" section . . . you can find any word you need at these sites!

Thesauri

You can even find a thesaurus online, at the following sites:

www.thesaurus.com

www.bartleby.com/62/

Writing Resources

webster.commnet.edu/mla.htm This site explains how to write a research paper using MLA style of documentation.

Resources for Teaching Writing

www.paragraphpunch.com/

www.essaypunch.com/

www.eduplace.com/rdg/hme/graphorg/toc.html

http://oswego.org/staff/caswell/wg/index.htm

Math Resources

www.mathstories.com

www.mathleague.com/help/help.htm

www.teach-nology.com/worksheets/math/

www.edhelper.com/

www.visualfractions.com/

www.mathgoodies.com/

Art Resources

www.metmuseum.org/   The Metropolitan Museum, NYC.

www.Paris.org/Musees/Louvre/   The Louvre Museum's official site.

www.thinker.org/fam/thinker.html   Fine Arts Museum, San Francisco—over 50,000 works on paper.

artsedge.kennedy-center.org/   This site has great lessons and teachers aides.

www.ibiblio.org/wm/paint   This is a "Famous Paintings Exhibit."

www.ibiblio-org/wm/paris/   A tour of Paris.

www.ibiblio.org/wm/paint/auth/cezanne   An exhibit of Cezanne—this is just one of many such exhibits at ibiblio.org. Check it out!

www.ibiblio.org Library of art.

www.kn.pacbell/wired/art2/index.html   Eyes on art, resources for teachers.

Foreign Language Resources

www.geocities.com/TheTropics/Island/9069/ConjugationTrainer/presbasic.html#manual

www.studyspanish.com/

www.linguaweb.ndirect.co.uk/pages/whichlan.htm

polyglot.lss.wisc.edu/lss/lang/langlink.html

babelfish.altavista.com/tr

www.weston.org/conjuguemos/

www.japaneselesson.com

www.itp.berkeley.edu/~thorne/HumanResources.html

Civics Resources

bensguide.gpo.gov/ This kids' site explains the three branches of the federal government, checks and balances, the election process, how laws are made, the Constitution, and so on.

www.usdoj.gov/kidspage/ The Department of Justice has a fascinating kids' site. It tells about the FBI's history, famous cases, investigation techniques such as fingerprinting and DNA testing, and much more.

www.odci.gov/cia/ciakids/index.html This site has fascinating facts about the CIA, intelligence gathering, spies, and more.

History Resources

www.historycentral.com/index.html This site has chronologies of world history, biographies of influential people of the twentieth century, histories of elections, railroads, aviation, American wars, and much more.

http://history.searchbeat.com This site has many timelines for different time periods and parts of the world, as well as timelines for specific historical events.

sunsite.utk.edu/civil-war/

guardians.net/egypt/ This site is packed with interesting information about ancient Egypt and includes a kids' section with lots of games and projects.

Geography

www.enchantedlearning.com/geography/flags   This site has many flag-coloring book pages.

www.eduplace.com/ss   The social studies center has current events, history update, and a geography game for kids.

library.thinkquest.org/10157/geoglobe.html   Interactive geography games!

Science Resources

www.brainpop.com   This site has dozens of animated movies on health, science, and technology topics that are geared for kids.

Resources for Teaching Kids with ADHD and/or Learning Disabilities

www.westfieldacademy.org/adhd/   Teaching tips from a home-schooling mom.

www.ldonline.org/   This site has tips for teaching kids with various learning disabilities—ADD/ADHD—and links to many organizations and resources.

www.schwablearning.org/

Scope and Sequence

Grade 1

Language Arts

Recognizing sounds of vowels and consonants, learning sight words, and reading names, labels, and signs.

Writing the entire alphabet and spelling simple words.

Introduction to nouns, verbs, and adjectives, punctuation, and capitalization.

Telling stories, dramatic plays, presenting information orally to a group, participating in group discussions, enunciation, and pronunciation.

Using table of contents.

Organizing ideas and writing simple stories, poems, and book reports.

Mathematics

Counting and writing numbers through 100, counting by twos up to 40, concept of ordinal and cardinal numbers, and number patterns.

Simple addition and subtraction facts including those using zero, solving simple word problems.

Number lines, place value, chance and probability, estimation, charts and graphs.

Time-telling, calendar use.

Value of coins, English and metric system measurement.

Understanding the concepts of equal, unequal, quantity, size, ½, and ¼.

Geometric figures.

Science

Living and nonliving things, types of animals such as insects and birds, habitats.

How animals are helpful, pets, zoo animals.

What plants need to grow, seeds, bulbs, flowers.

Weather and seasons, air, air pollution, wind.

The moon, sun, and other stars, planets, day and night.

Fossil fuels, bodies of water, mountains, and valleys.

Three states of matter, heat, temperature, sound, and light.

Magnets, machines, and movement.

Scientific method and inquiry, performing simple experiments and recording results, and classification of objects.

Our five senses, keeping our bodies healthy and safe.

Social Studies

Holidays, traditions, and customs.

American flag, symbols, and freedoms.

Past cultures.

Families, neighborhoods, and communities, community helpers, social skills and responsibilities, jobs, and careers.

Farms and zoos.

Basic geography terms, making simple maps.

Grade 2

Language Arts

Reading poetry with appreciation, reading charts to get information, predicting what happens next in narratives, reading silently, oral reading, and vocabulary acquisition.

Following written directions.

Spelling and word attack skills.

Homonyms, synonyms, antonyms, punctuation and capitalization, quotation marks.

Organizing ideas and writing stories with a beginning, a middle, and an end, using description, and writing simple letters, journal entries, and poems.

Using tables of contents and indexes of books, using dictionary guide words, and alphabetizing by using the first and second letters of words.

Mathematics

Counting, reading, and writing numbers through 1000, and counting by 2s, 3s, 4s, 5s, and 10s.

Counting to 10 with ordinal numbers.

Addition and subtraction facts to 20, basic multiplication and division, multiplying with zero and one, understanding relationship between addition and subtraction and between multiplication and division.

Understanding 1s, 10s, and 100s places and use of 0 to hold a place.

Practical use of basic fractions, understanding the concept of ratio.

Time-telling and using the calendar, counting coins, common English and metric measurements.

Geometry puzzles and activities.

Using charts and graphs, estimation, using sets.

Science

Scientific method and inquiry, making graphs.

Sun, moon, planets, constellations, space exploration, gravity.

Magnets, machines, and forces, light and mirrors, heat, sound, electricity, and using it safely.

Earth, sky, air, weather, and how it affects Earth, water cycle, rivers, oceans, water and air pollution, and climate.

Dinosaurs and other extinct animals.

Habitats, life cycle, plant reproduction and growth, bulbs, seeds, leaf cuttings, how plants make their food.

Food chain, animal food, how animals defend themselves, how seasons affect animals and plants.

Birds, mammals, reptiles, amphibians, and insects, baby animals.

Social Studies

Holidays and traditions.

Patriotic celebrations and observances, our nation's capital and American landmarks, Pledge of Allegiance.

Families, neighborhoods, and communities, families and communities around the world.

Working, earning, and spending money on goods and services, and paying taxes, community services, and community helpers.

Interdependence of people, working cooperatively, laws, citizenship, and social responsibility.

Concept of history, family history, Christopher Columbus, Pilgrims coming to the New World, Powhatan tribe and Pocahontas, Jamestown settlement, 13 colonies, Declaration of Independence, American Revolution and a few founding fathers, and pioneers heading westward.

Map and globe skills including the four basic directions, locating continents, and identifying the United States and its states.

Understanding land form maps and identifying geographical features such as mountains, islands, peninsulas, rivers, and lakes.

Grade 3

Language Arts

Beginning cursive writing, writing short stories and poems, editing and proofreading work.

Silent reading, developing word attack skills, reading aloud, orally recounting experiences accurately and in correct sequence.

Using a dictionary, alphabetizing using the first three letters of the words, using indexes.

Synonyms, antonyms, homonyms, spelling, paragraphs, using periods, commas, question marks, apostrophes, and quotation marks.

Mathematics

Reading and writing numbers up to 10,000.

Beginning Roman numerals.

Addition and subtraction facts to 25.

Multiplication and division facts through 100.

Rounding and estimation, simple fractions, practical applications of positive and negative numbers.

Numeration systems.

Perimeter, area, volume, properties of solid figures, geometric constructions, and similar and congruent figures.

Time-telling to the nearest minute.

Word problems.

Charts and graphs.

Science

Scientific method and inquiry.

Desert animals, forest animals, sea animals, dinosaurs, working animals.

Birds, trees, flowers, and forest plants.

Animal and plant conservation, and life cycle.

Moon and stars, gravity, and satellites of Earth.

Weather and climate and how Earth's surface changes.

Magnets and compasses, sources of energy, electricity, light and color, forces, work, and machines.

Social Studies

Holidays and customs, and understanding of different faiths, cultures, and races.

Native Americans, explorers, and pioneers.

History of transportation and communication.

Citizenship and social responsibility, history and development of local community, community helpers.

Human's basic needs and how they are met, consumers and producers of goods, sources of food, clothing, and shelter.

Maps and globes, continents, U.S. geography, local geography.

Grade 4

Language Arts

Silent reading, oral reading, and choral reading, and listening skills.

Reading short stories, chapter books, poetry and plays for enjoyment, critical reading.

Learning to locate information using indexes, encyclopedias, and newspapers.

Writing letters, summaries of simple information, outlines, book reports, and creative works.

Telephone manners and skills, social introductions.

Mathematics

Reading and writing numbers.

Roman numerals up to C.

Prime numbers and prime factoring.

Numeration systems.

Subsets.

Addition and subtraction of numbers with as many as seven digits, multiplication and division facts to 144, multiplying numbers with up to three digits, dividing two- and three-digit numbers by one-digit numbers.

Understanding relationship between fractions and decimals and understanding concept of mixed numbers.

Time-telling to the nearest second and English and metric measurement.

Charts and graphs, finding averages.

Geometric concepts.

Science

Scientific method and inquiry, solar system, universe, and living in space.

Earth and its history and prehistoric plants and animals.

Oceans, weather's effects on the Earth, and meteorology, cause of seasons, and climate.

Ecosystems and balance of nature.

Classification of living things, insects and reptiles.

Plant structure and function.

Magnets, electricity, light and color.

Environment and pollution.

Human body.

Biological organization.

Social Studies

Using maps and globes and understanding longitude, latitude, and scale, continents, and time zones.

World regions, climate regions, Earth's resources, and world cultures.

History of the formation of your state, your state's place in its region, country, and world.

Grade 5

Language Arts

Writing outlines, paragraphs, letters, stories, poems, plays, and reports with bibliographies, and proofreading work, and spelling.

Using dictionary and thesaurus, and locating information using tables of contents, indexes, graphs, charts, and tables, and library catalogue or computer database.

Silent reading, reading newspapers, oral reading, and presenting original plays.

Understanding the different types of literature.

Homophones, homographs, synonyms, and antonyms.

Types of sentences, sentence parts, plurals, and possessives.

Mathematics

Reading and writing numbers up to 10 digits.

Set of integers, numeration systems.

Addition, subtraction, multiplication, and division of whole numbers.

Fundamental processes; whole numbers and common fractions.

Fractions, mixed numbers, and decimals to the thousandths place.

Ratio and percent.

Exponents.

English and metric measurement.

Geometric concepts.

Practical word problems.

Concept of sampling, charts, picture graphs, bar graphs, and circle graphs.

Science

Scientific method and scientific inquiry.

Magnetic fields, light and optics, electricity, force systems, and chemical systems.

Social Studies

Exploration and settlement in the New World, life in the American colonies, the American Revolution, and concepts of freedom and democracy and relevant documents.

Westward expansion and pioneer life.

U.S. geography, life in the United States and in its possessions, and natural resources of the United States.

The neighbors of the United States, Canada, and Mexico, and the different cultures in Canada.

Using maps and globes.

Western hemisphere countries and cultures.

Grade 6

Language Arts

Reading silently and skimming for main points, and reading critically.

Acquiring familiarity with types of literature including mythology, lyric poetry, narrative poetry, and dramatic poetry.

Acquiring familiarity with types of writing including narration, description, exposition, and persuasion.

Cursive handwriting.

Sentence structure, nouns, pronouns, verbs, adjectives, and adverbs, and diagraming sentences.

Vocabulary acquisition, spelling, homonyms, synonyms, and antonyms, roots, prefixes, and suffixes.

Note-taking, writing outlines, letters, reports, bibliographies, news articles, poetry in verse, and stories.

Organization of a book.

Using a dictionary, locating information from indexes, reference books, and electronic reference materials.

Listening and nonverbal communication.

Mathematics

Exponents and operations involving them.

Set of integers.

Factoring.

Fundamental operations with fractions and decimals, fundamental operations with compound denominate numbers, multiplying and dividing with mixed numbers and fractions.

Relationship between decimals and fractions, percents.

Geometric figures and their properties, constructing geometric figures, measuring angles, recognizing similarity, congruence, and symmetry.

Scale drawings.

English and metric measurement.

Averaging numbers, understanding the concept of sampling.

Using calculators and computers.

Analyzing problems.

Obtaining information from graphs.

Science

Scientific theory.

Inventions and discoveries.

Astronomy, universe and space, and space travel.

Elements and compounds.

Magnetism, electricity, radioactivity and nuclear energy, solar and geothermal energy.

Sound, light, and heat.

Classification of living things, microbes, algae, and fungi.

Ecosystems, ecology and the environment, conservation, recycling.

Geology, oceans, climate, and weather

Human body, food for growth and energy.

Social Studies

Using maps and globes, world geography, countries and regions of the world and their cultures.

Relationships among countries, international trade, transportation, and communication.

Citizenship and social responsibility.

Native American cultures.

Milestones in human achievement.

The Roman Empire.

Grade 7

Language Arts

Acquiring familiarity with different types of poetry, novels, short stories, plays, myths, legends, ballads, biography and autobiography, and literary terms.

Listening skills.

Using a dictionary, locating information in atlases, encyclopedias, periodicals, and from Internet sources.

Parts of speech, clauses and phrases, compound sentences.

Punctuation in speech, speech activities.

Taking notes, writing outlines, reports, letters, and journal entries, writing descriptively.

Mathematics

Prime numbers, composite numbers.

Geometry concepts and terms.

Perimeter, circumference, and area, using formulas, metric and English measurement.

Use of calculators and computers, business math.

Working with graphs, understanding the concepts of mean, mode, median, and range.

Properties of nonnegative integers, ratio and proportion.

Rational numbers.

Fractions, percents.

Square roots.

Order of operations.

Numeration.

Absolute value, inequalities.

Science

Scientific classification

Cells, genetics.

Rocks and minerals, soil, and effects of weather on them.

Atmosphere and air pressure.

Scientific method, laboratory techniques and safety.

Ecology and the environment, conservation.

Properties of water.

Laws of motion.

Energy, heat and temperature.

Social Studies

Eastern Hemisphere countries and cultures.

Prehistoric people, ancient civilizations of Greece, Rome, and the Middle East.

The Middle Ages, the Renaissance, the Reformation.

Scientific Revolution, Age of Reason, Industrial Age.

The past and present of Europe, Asia, the Middle East, Australia, and the Pacific.

World geography, using maps and globes.

Contemporary problems and issues, environment.

International trade and resources.

Grade 8

Language Arts

Infinitives, gerunds, direct objects, indirect objects, participles, predicate nominatives, and predicate adjectives.

Types of sentences and their parts.

Reading nonfiction, novels, short stories, poetry, biographies of great Americans, and prose and poetry by American authors.

Literary terms and figures of speech.

Inductive and deductive reasoning, inferential, literal, and evaluative reading skills.

Dramatics, listening and speech activities.

Writing business letters and reports.

Using a dictionary and other reference materials.

Spelling and vocabulary acquisition.

Mathematics

Maintaining skills in fundamental operations.

Factoring.

Working with fractions, decimals, percent, ratio and proportion.

Formulas and equations, graphing equations.

Polynomials.

Probability statistics and statistical terms.

Mathematics of insurance, taxes, and banking.

Permutations.

Metric and nonmetric geometry, Pythagorean theorem.

Right-triangle trigonometry.

Scale drawing.

Powers and roots of rational numbers.

Numeration systems.

Sets and simple sentences.

English and metric measurement.

Science

Scientific method, scientific nomenclature, scientific measurement.

Ecology and the environment, conservation, recycling of resources.

Composition of the Earth.

Weather.

Weathering and erosion.

Astronomy, the universe and the Milky Way galaxy, space and space travel.

The periodic table of the elements, atoms, molecules, compounds and mixtures, chemical changes, forces in liquids and gases.

Water and its uses, ocean, atmosphere.

The Earth's movement.

Newton's three laws of motion.

Machines.

Wave energy, mechanical energy, electrical energy, and nuclear energy, magnetism and electricity, heat and light.

Social Studies

Geography, political system, economic system, and the government of the United States.

American culture, democracy.

Using maps and globes.

Our African, Asian, and European heritages.

Exploration of the New World.

Life in the American colonies, American Revolution, U.S. Constitution.

Westward expansion and pioneers.

American Civil War and Reconstruction.

United States as a world power.

Grade 9

Language Arts

Public speaking, debate, listening skills, and discussion.

Vocabulary including foreign words used in English.

Basics of composition, grammar.

Honing skills in using reference materials, writing reports.

Reading newspapers, propaganda, and advertisements, and evaluating them.

Interpretation of literature, parables and allegories, poetry.

Reading folklore, myths, novels, short stories, dramatic poetry.

Drama, film, structure of a play.

Mathematics

General mathematics or algebra 1

Science

Astronomy, space and space travel.

Atomic structure, molecular theory, chemistry of matter, chemicals and their uses, metals and plastics.

Light and its uses, solar energy.

Nuclear energy, heat and fuels.

Electricity, electronics.

History of the Earth, earth science, erosion, climates.

Ecology and the environment, air pollution, water pollution, water and its uses.

Weather, air and air pressure, air masses and fronts.

Disease and its causes.

Social Studies

Conservation (including human conservation), resource management.

Using maps and globes, world geography.

American democracy, U.S. Constitution, political parties and elections, taxation.

Basic economics, labor and management, labor unions.

Community, state, and national governments, rights and responsibilities of U.S. citizens.

Comparative cultures and religions, ethnic studies.

United Nations.

Urban studies.

Basic human communities.

Grade 10

Language Arts

History of alphabet and writing.

Using dictionaries.

Vocabulary and etymology, geographical dialects.

Writing techniques, persuasion and argumentation, grammar.

Writing short stories, plays, poetry, journal entries, and term papers with footnotes.

Listening skills, debate, and public speaking.

Distinguishing fact from opinion.

American literature including novel short stories and essays, folklore, and ballads.

Literature from other cultures.

Interpretation and critique of literature.

Reading lyric poetry and sonnets.

Drama.

Mathematics

Origins and uses of geometry.

The nature of proof, inductive and deductive reasoning.

Geometry terms, postulates, and theorems.

Sets.

Ratio and proportion.

Algebra in geometry.

Polygons, relationship between circles and polygons.

Parallel and perpendicular lines.

Angle relationships.

Measurement of geometric figures.

Circles, congruent triangles, right triangles, Pythagorean Theorem.

Simple constructions.

Loci.

Coordinate geometry.

Introduction to symbolic logic.

Problem solving with geometry.

Trigometric functions of angles greater than 90 degrees.

Transformational geometry.

Science

Scientific method.

Characteristics of living things, history of plants and animals.

Classification of living things, algae, bacteria and fungi, vertebrates, mammals and birds.

Disease-causing microorganisms.

Human biology, digestive system, growth and reproduction behavior.

Cells, DNA-RNA, protein synthesis, genetics and heredity, genetic engineering.

Plants, photosynthesis.

Space travel and biology.

Energy in ecosystems, environmental issues, conservation of human resources.

Social Studies

Prehistoric people, ancient civilizations of India, China, the Islamic world, and Greece.

The Middle Ages, African civilizations, civilizations in the Americas.

The Renaissance, monarchies, birth of modern democracy, French Revolution.

Nationalism, Imperialism.

The Industrial Revolution, scientific advances.

World War I, the Great Depression, World War II, democratic ideals and values.

The Cold War, the Vietnam War, the rise and fall of communism, the collapse of the Soviet Union.

Global issues, role of women around the world.

Grade 11

Language Arts

Mass communication, propaganda techniques, advertising, critical and evaluative reading.

Writing stories, editorials, news stories, writing term papers, proof-reading symbols.

Vocabulary acquisition, grammar.

American literature, literature of other cultures, analysis of plays, poetry terms.

Use of *Reader's Guide* and other references materials.

Music, painting, architecture, and sculpture.

Listening skills.

Mathematics

Algebra II or trigonometry

Science

Matter and its behavior, atomic theory, molecular theory.

Carbon and organic compounds, metals and alloys, nonmetals.

Formulas and chemical equations, chemical bonding, chemical changes, acids, bases, and salts.

Water and solutions, ionization and ionic solutions, colloids, suspensoids, and emulsoids.

Titrations.

Oxidation-reduction, electrochemistry.

Periodic law.

Forms of energy, equilibrium and kinetics, spontaneous reactions.

Measurement.

Nuclear reactions and radioactivity.

Social Studies

Exploration of the New World.

American colonies, the birth of the United States of America, U.S. Constitution.

Nationalism.

Sectionalism.

American Civil War and Reconstruction.

Struggle for women's rights, role of women in society today.

World War I, the Great Depression, World War II.

The Cold War and nuclear era.

Civil rights movement.

Public education.

Societal problems including crime, problems of mental health.

Psychology.

Urbanization.

Grade 12

Language Arts

English literature, Shakespeare, political, social, and literary history of England.

Parliamentary procedures.

Listening skills.

Identifying verbals.

Twentieth-century literature, world literature, literature of other cultures.

Current periodical literature, critical and evaluative reading.

Tragedy and comedy, the theater, film, acting.

Mass communication, comparative study of mass media, radio and television.

Writing reports, term papers, and bibliographies, social and business letters, book reviews, essays.

Mathematics

Calculus or advanced algebra

Science

Physics.

Electricity and magnetism.

Photoelectric effect.

Heat.

Light and optics.

Sound and acoustics.

Wave motion.

Quantum theory.

Relativity.

Force.

Mechanics.

Space, time, and motion.

Work, energy, and power.

Electronics.

Nuclear energy.

Nuclear physics.

Solid-state physics.

Social Studies

Democratic ideals, principles of U.S. government, important U.S. documents, American political party system.

U.S. agriculture, business and industry in the United States, taxation and finance.

Economic theories and concepts, comparative economic systems, distribution and exchange of goods and services, labor and management.

American foreign policy, international relations, international organizations.

Public education.

Comparative systems of government.

Urbanization.

Crime.

Conservation.

Consumer education.

Psychology.

The role of women in society today.

Family economics and management.

Glossary

ACT: The American College Testing Assessment, which is used to help determine a high school student's readiness for college.

Classical homeschooling: An approach based on the trivium, which divides education into three stages. First there is the grammar stage, during which children learn to read and write and learn facts. Then during the early teenage years, they begin learning to think abstractly. In the last stage, called the rhetoric stage, the teen puts together what has been learned and learns to write and speak well.

Colfax, David and Micki: In the late 1980s, this homeschooling couple and four boys made the national news when their oldest son was admitted to Harvard, and they have written popular books about their homeschooling experiences.

Deschooling: An adjustment period that a child goes through after being removed from a conventional classroom setting into home-schooling.

Eclectic approach: A patchwork of a variety of homeschooling approaches created by an individual homeschooling family to meet their children's educational needs.

Educational Resources Information Center (ERIC): A national information system containing the largest education database in the world.

Gatto, John Taylor: After teaching in the New York City public school system for over three decades, he became a vocal critic of public schools and an advocate of homeschooling.

GED (general education development) testing: An alternative to a traditional high school diploma. It is used by high school dropouts wishing to complete their high school education, but also by many homeschoolers in lieu of a diploma.

Hirsch, E.D.: An influential author known for his ideas of cultural literacy and for his Core Knowledge Series.

Holt, John: An advocate of homeschooling who in the late 1970s began publishing *Growing Without Schooling*, an unschooling magazine still in circulation today. He authored numerous books in which he elaborated on his ideas that children learn best when they are allowed to learn what interests them. Unschooling families incorporate many of his ideas into their homeschooling.

Homeschool cooperative: A group of homeschooling families who join together to share resources. They might share school materials, operate a homeschooling library for its members, do team teaching, or work together in any number of ways to further their mutual goal of educating their children.

Homeschool Legal Defense Association (HSLDA): This organization was founded in 1983 by attorneys who took on the challenge of making homeschooling legal in every state. A decade later that goal was accomplished, but HSLDA continues to challenge homeschooling laws that it feels are overly restrictive or vague. They also help many homeschooling parents whose right to homeschool is unlawfully interfered with by local officials.

Homeschool support group: A group of homeschooling families who meet regularly and usually provide opportunities for homeschooling parents to share ideas and experiences with other homeschooling parents. This also allows homeschooled kids to get to know other homeschooled kids and to do activities as a group.

Individual educational plan (IEP): When children with learning disabilities are identified through the public school system's evaluation, a team, together with the child's parents, formulates this plan tailored to meet the child's needs.

Iowa Test of Basic Skills (ITBS): A standardized test used by many homeschooling families to comply with state testing requirements or for other purposes.

Mason, Charlotte, approach: This is a way of homeschooling based on the writings of Charlotte Mason, who in the nineteenth century wrote a book about home education from a Christian perspective. It involves having children read a lot of good literature, recite things that are read to them, and observe and record things in nature. It avoids using what Mason referred to as "twaddle," that is, poor-quality reading materials containing only superficial information.

Montessori homeschooling: An approach based on the ideas of Dr. Maria Montessori, which emphasizes the importance of making the environment and learning materials readily accessible to children and allows the child to learn at his or her own pace.

Moore, Dr. Raymond and Dorothy: Homeschooling writers who believe that it is best to delay formal instruction until children are 8 to 10 years old.

The National Home Education Network (NHEN): This organization's mission is to encourage and facilitate the work of state and local homeschooling groups and individuals.

National Home Education Research Institute (NHERI): A nonprofit organization that serves as a clearinghouse of research for home-schoolers, researchers, and policy makers. It also educates the public about homeschooling research findings.

Phonics-based reading instruction: Methods of teaching reading that teach the sounds represented by the letters of the alphabet and their combinations and then teach the blending of individual sounds to read words.

School-at-home approach: A way of homeschooling that closely imitates the traditional routines and methods of public schools.

Scope and sequence: What topics are taught in which grades.

Special needs students: Children who need some sort of extra help or modification of their usual school routines due to learning disabilities.

Support school: *See* umbrella programs.

Teaching across the curriculum: Teaching lessons that span several subjects.

Trivium: *See* classical education.

Umbrella program: A program allowing homeschoolers to operate as if they are part of the conventional school. They may provide traditional curricula and testing, or may just function as a record-keeping service. Some homeschoolers use them to simplify compliance with their states' laws.

Unit studies: An integration of all or most school subjects into a single study revolving around a topic.

Unschooling: A homeschooling approach strongly influenced by the ideas of John Holt. Central to unschooling is the notion that a child's natural curiosity and desire to participate in the adult world will eventually lead the child to learn all that he or she needs to know. The unschooling parent acts as a facilitator who helps the child pursue the subjects the child wishes to explore without dictating what the child will learn and when.

Waldorf homeschooling: An approach to education based on a school founded by Rudolf Steiner in the early twentieth century. Waldorf programs encourage a child's imagination and creativity. Homeschooling families who follow this approach find that a lot of its ways of teaching various subjects are great fun for both parent and child.

Whole-language reading instruction: A method of reading instruction that de-emphasizes the decoding of words phonetically and immerses the child in reading and related activities.

Index

About the Authors

Laura Saba is a former public school teacher, and has been successfully home-schooling her children for six years.

Julie Gattis is a registered nurse and occasional lecturer. She has seven years of homeschooling experience.

Dr. Lawrence Rudner is director of the Educational Resources Information Center (ERIC) Clearinghouse on Assessment and Evaluation, operated by the United States Department of Education's Office of Educational Research and Improvement. A former public school mathematics teacher, Dr. Rudner has held positions at the National Institute of Education and the Office of Educational Research and Development. His work has been published extensively in scholarly journals, and recently he has coedited the book *What Teachers Should Know about Testing*. In 1999 the findings of his groundbreaking research on the achievement levels of homeschooled students were reported in all major newspapers and resulted in his appearance on C-SPAN.